GLOAMING

Rosie
Steer

Folklore, recipes + crafts

to spark glimmers of joy

in the darker months

BLOOMSBURY PUBLISHING
LONDON • OXFORD • NEW YORK • NEW DELHI • SYDNEY

To Al & Laurie

Gentle snowflakes dancing
in the breeze.

Frost
sparkling on distant rooftops.

A winter sky, the perfect periwinkle blue.

Pine needles
and woodsmoke.

A sunset
in soft shades of
lilac and apricot.

Glimmers
of light
glistening through
ominous clouds,
illuminating the sky
for an instant.

INTRODUCTION

Winter can often look and feel magical in all its Christmas-card, snow-frosted beauty, and yet, for every romanticised version of winter, there is the darker reality: the howl of wind down the chimney; the endless grey of a restless winter sky; the crashing of waves against the shore; the lashing of rain on the windows; treacherous ice underfoot.

It's no wonder so many of us struggle with the winter months. The NHS estimates that approximately 2 million people in the UK and 12 million people in Northern Europe experience seasonal affective disorder (SAD) every year, a type of seasonal depression more prevalent in winter, thought to be linked to reduced exposure to sunlight during the darker months. While many live without a diagnosis, there is no doubt that lots of us find this period incredibly difficult, and inevitably end up counting down the days until spring. The darker half of the year lasts from September to March – so that's half our lives we are wishing away, hoping our fortunes fare better when the days are lighter and longer. I know I have often wished away the winter months, then put so much pressure on spring and summer that they don't live up to my rose-tinted expectations. The world keeps turning, and then I'm plunged into darkness again, still unsatisfied, still wanting, still not fully present.

Contemporary conveniences shelter many of us from the true harshness of winter; however, they also mask our circadian rhythms, and the needs of our bodies and minds for slower times of rest and rejuvenation. This, along with societal pressures – from the relentless pace of the modern working world to the consumerism that has taken over ancient holidays – can lead us to feel we should be going about our lives like we're in some perpetual summer. I know there have been times where I have felt so out of touch with nature's patterns and cycles, unable to step off the treadmill of life and surrender to the once instinctive rhythm of the year.

But maybe there's another way we can look at this cycle of darkness and light? A way we can learn to make the most of the season we're in. To embed time in nature and creative pursuits into our autumn and winter routines. To give ourselves permission to slow down and find moments of joy. To let in both light and dark.

The arrival of 'nychtin-time' – the Scots word for the dark half of the year – signals a slowing down in nature, an over-wintering or hibernation. The season invites us to turn inwards and homewards. My Scottish ancestors understood this rhythm so deeply that it informed the very language they spoke, which eventually evolved into the contemporary Scots language, replete with many terms for snow, rain, darkness and nighttime. Scots even beats the Inuit languages in terms of the number of different words for snow, totalling more than 400 different terms, according to researchers at the University of Glasgow. 'Sneesl' (to begin to rain or snow), 'feefle' (to swirl), 'snaw-pouther' (light, driving snow) and 'unbrak' (the beginning of a thaw) are just a few of my favourite examples.

Many Scots weather words evoke the harshness of the darker months (and even sound harsh): 'smuir' (misty/hazy), 'blyte' (a blast of bad weather), 'brattle' (a sudden spell of inclement weather) and 'pusker' (storm). Probably the most well-known Scots weather word – 'dreich' – summons up a particular kind of weather that almost goes beyond translation, the word for the dreary, depressing weather uniquely experienced on a November day in Edinburgh. The kind of day where it's not really raining, but it's definitely not dry, and you end up cold and soaked to the skin.

It is clear to me that the weather and seasons have formed an essential part of our lives and identities for hundreds of years in Scotland, the language being a vital way to communicate all the different types of weather – especially bad – that could shape livelihoods and lives, particularly in winter. In our modern world, we seem to have forgotten that times of darkness are as much a part of nature's rhythms as they are a part of life – but I know from experience that this healthier, more mindful approach is far easier talked about than put into practice. Instead, we understandably try to push it away and ignore it: we put on an extra light and layer, take our vitamin D, binge another TV series, book a summer holiday and fritter away time until the spring.

In my late twenties, I reached breaking point on the treadmill of life and reconnecting with nature was something that helped to heal me. When I was diagnosed with OCD, anxiety and depression, I found solace in the certainty of the rhythms of the year, and the creative projects they could inspire. And yet, even as someone who writes about the healing power of living slowly and seasonally, I was soon to find that these were lessons I would need to learn over and over, when one winter I was plunged into my own 'nychtin-time' – a deeper than ever period of difficulty – when I found out that I was pregnant with our much longed-for baby. I didn't feel how I thought I would, or how I thought I should. Instead of glowing and nesting joyfully, embracing my bump and planning a cosy nursery like the mums I saw on Instagram, I was paralysed by anxiety.

My pregnancy sickness arrived with winter's storms and the intrusive thoughts of my OCD that I had recently learned to manage went into overdrive as I imagined all the different ways that I could harm the baby. I would need to perform endless compulsions of checking, cleaning and reassurance-seeking in a fruitless attempt to placate my anxiety.

On the surface, I kept functioning as 'normal', too scared to tell anyone – even my husband, Al – the extent of these thoughts; inside, I was falling apart. Despite healthy scans, I was terrified that I would lose the baby.

To cope, I went back to masking – something I was adept at from years of hiding my anxiety. But this time the contrast between my inner turmoil and outward coping was even more profound. I was now a 'Successful Author'. My book was a bestseller. My workshops around the book's launch sold out in less than forty-eight hours. People wanted to meet me. Meanwhile, I was in the midst of the busiest term as a teacher and drowning in marking and reports. I was waxing lyrical in my workshops about slow living, about nurturing our minds through nature and giving ourselves permission to create – and then going straight home to bed, burnt out.

A reader at one event spoke to me about their mental health, asked how I really was and what was next. I was privileged to hear she had given *Slow Seasons* to a friend going through IVF and was brought much comfort by it. I said to her then, 'We need *Even Slower Seasons.*' I started to wonder if I could help even more people if I was honest enough with myself.

As the days began to lengthen, help eventually arrived in the form of my NHS therapist, Melanie. As well as working through cognitive behavioural therapy (CBT) strategies and supporting me by writing an emotionally informed birth plan together, she introduced me to 'glimmers', a term coined by social worker Deb Dana who found that searching for these micro-moments of joy actually makes us feel happier. Looking for and actively noting these moments allows our bodies and brains to regulate and feel connected, which in turn enables our nervous systems to make us feel calm, safe and hopeful.

I'll be honest, I was a little cynical as I felt more anxious than I ever had done – the sense of responsibility that came with my OCD, heightened by the reality of growing a child, left me on high alert and feeling incredibly lonely and low as a result. The idea that small joys could solve this deep depression seemed impossible, but I was desperate to try anything that would help, and started searching for slivers of light this way. I made a concerted effort to write down three good things each day in a note on my phone, which at first felt like an enormous effort. Although I had written for so long about searching for positive moments in each season,

'But maybe there's
another way we can
look at this cycle of
darkness & light?
A way we can learn
to make the most
of the season
we're in.'

I felt like I was starting again from scratch, re-learning slow and simple living. I began to self-medicate in the only ways I knew how – by turning to nature, getting outside and nourishing my body and mind with comforting bakes and wholesome crafts. At last, I felt able to reconnect with the seasonal joys I had written about for so long that felt so distant in the depths of winter darkness.

And yet, while I was beginning to replenish my stocks of inspiration, a key thing still niggled at me: I struggled to write. The blank page overwhelmed me, and documenting my matrescence seemed unthinkable. Pregnancy was beyond words, beyond articulation.

At times when I have previously struggled to find the language to write about my experiences, I turned to the words of my ancestors instead. Scots words. I became intrigued by the many Scots words associated with darkness, particularly terms used to describe the darkest parts of the day and the year: 'dounsetting' (the setting of the sun), 'forenicht' (the early part of the night) and the 'head of the dim' (midnight). I could go on and on. Clearly, we Scots are obsessed with the mirk – the darkness – and with an hour less daylight in Midwinter (mid-December) compared to our neighbours in the south (around seven hours in Edinburgh versus London's eight) it's maybe easy to see why. On the flipside, I soon realised that there were also many words around finding the light – the 'achening' (early dawn), 'scarrow' (faint light), 'skimmers' (flickering rays), 'scraigh-o'day' (dawn's first appearance), 'glisk' (a gleam of sunlight through a cloud) and so on – that reminded me of the balance in the natural world.

One Scots word in particular stood out to me: 'gloamin'' or 'gloaming' [n] – the word for evening dusk or morning daybreak, especially in autumn and winter. Half-light, twilight. The word seemed to encapsulate the particular beauty and savouring of the light when it is found in the darker months. A warm, dusky and romantic light that lingers just after sunset.

I realised that instead of focusing on fighting the darkness, I needed to accept it. To pay enough attention to spot those moments of passing lightness. This was what had sent me a lifeline over a long, hard winter without me realising: nature, small moments, even slower seasons. The more I noted them, the easier these moments became to find, and things began to feel more hopeful – or at least less immediately threatening, the baby less precarious. The anxiety hadn't disappeared, but I could live alongside it again by embracing Melanie's glimmers.

Going back to my ancestors offers a different perspective on the darker half of the year. The Celts' observance of micro-seasons offers an alternative way of marking nature's progress through the dark, an acknowledgement of the smallest seasonal shifts as the light wanes, then grows once more. There are various names in Scots for these smaller subdivisions within autumn and winter, including Hairst (harvest), Samhain (pronounced 'sah-wane', Hallowe'en), Howe o' the year (the winter solstice) and Waretym (earliest spring). I've chosen to structure this book around those smaller winter subdivisions as they not only accept the darkness in the knowledge that light will come again, but also honour and cherish it. Each chapter is divided into an introduction to the micro-season, stories from folklore associated with that time, and recipes and crafts to help you find the light and embrace the darkness during wintertime.

To me, there is a poetry in the Scots language and the traditions it encapsulates and evolved from, and there are lessons to be learned from these winter subdivisions, the tales of folklore that accompany them and the activities they inspire. Led by my ancestors, I look to nature to find the light in my own, modern context, every day. Whether that's baking something with the ingredients of the earth to pay homage to nature's bounty, preserving autumn leaves in beeswax to pause time for a while, retelling stories of Cailleach – Queen of Winter – and her temporary victory over the light, or noticing the very first spring flowers as the season turns and picking them to make an arrangement, this book aims to lead you to find your own glimmers through dark times and practice gratitude and self-compassion by actively seeking out and nurturing the small joys that the season provides if we look for them. In turn, these small but magical moments can help us make the most of the season we're in rather than wishing it away, allowing us to thrive in the light that lingers before total darkness, in the gloaming.

PART 1

HARVEST

START OF AUGUST

TO END OF OCTOBER

There's a golden tinge and growing haziness about the land as we turn the calendar to August.

As the days begin to tiptoe shorter, a gradual surrendering to the season's rhythm takes hold: a call from our ancestors to begin our preparations for wintertime. The light begins to change as the heat of late summer starts to break. The flowers, now past their peak, put on a final show. The hedgerows ripen, a growing glut of nuts and berries, hips and haws. Heather turns heath, moor and mountainside a dusky purple, and wild raspberries and blueberries (known in Scotland as blaeberries) are ready for the picking. Migrating birds like swifts, swallows and house martins prepare to depart, noisily gathering on rooftops and overhead wires, and knitwear calls to us from the back of the drawer as the mornings turn misty. The leaves start to turn from green to russet and gold. The gloaming's warm light softens the edges of the land as the sun slips below the horizon a little earlier every evening.

In the Celtic calendar, the arrival of harvest signifies the end of summer and the beginning of the darker half of the year in the seasonal cycle. Although the days have technically been reducing in length since Midsummer and the longest day around 21 June, the change becomes more noticeable as August mellows into September, days contracting gradually then suddenly all at once as we reach the autumn equinox on 22 or 23 September.

Change is in the air

I've sometimes found that the end of summer can bring with it a growing sense of grief. Here in Scotland, the new school year begins in mid-August (following an earlier start to the summer holidays at the end of June) so I've always associated these weeks with a significant turning point – especially as an English teacher still beholden to term time! I would often find myself mourning the dwindling light and freedoms of the warmer months, perhaps the projects unfinished, trips not taken and an unshakeable sense that maybe we haven't 'made the most of it' – whatever 'it' is. A feeling of time going too fast, opportunities disappearing, time running out.

In the past, to try and cope with this end of holiday anxiety, I would make myself extra busy by filling the diary with events, activities and trips as if summer would never return. It might seem obvious, but rather than helping me savour the moment it would do the opposite – adding to a feeling of overwhelm and self-inflicted pressure to complete an unrealistic summer 'bucket list'. When you try to force enjoyment, it seldom happens.

Instead, I now make a conscious effort to see this transitional time differently. I sit with the feelings, rather than try to escape them. I feel the sadness and accept the anxiety of time's passing and summer's farewell, but I also look to Mother Nature for her cues to savour the abundance around us and to embrace this in-between time, as there is richness and plenty to be found if we honour the seasonal shift rather than try to resist it. In recent years I've come to look for nature's signs as an invitation to slow down, to linger a little longer in the light, to ground ourselves in the here and now and be intentional with the fruits of our harvest as we head into the colder months. It might be spotting hedgehogs in green spaces at dusk, hunting for food before they hibernate, or noticing bees and wasps getting slower and sillier, perhaps even finding their way into the warmth inside. The trees offer certain signs, whether on countryside lanes or in city parks: the green acorns on oak trees are beginning to turn brown, and the conkers are falling, while the leaves of the canopy and on exposed branches are beginning to turn – first the horse chestnut, then the sycamore and birch trees.

Rather than a countdown timer marking an inevitable descent into winter, this summer to autumn transition can be viewed as a time to look forward to and enjoy. I try to hold on to the new season energy that is the other side of that back-to-school feeling: of freshly polished shoes, sharpened pencils, maybe a new notebook and project to enjoy. The arrival of harvest season means getting out my favourite knitwear, like greeting old friends; it's restocking the candles and appreciating their homely glow as the nights begin to draw in; it's delighting in trips to our local grocer for autumn produce, then coming home and enjoying comforting bowl food once again; it's trips to the woods to revel in the childish magic of the changing leaves.

The activities in this chapter aim to savour the small joys within these moments and preserve them, as I turn to my ancestors for their seasonal wisdom. If long Scottish winters have taught me anything, it's that being present in the here and now is vital – not dreading the passage from light to dark, long days to short, or getting out the hardiest winter layers too soon! I also find that bottling up a little of August and September's abundance helps me to engage all my senses in the here and now – preparing my ingredients, slowly stirring simmering pots of jams and chutneys, testing for the setting point and decanting them into jars – with the added bonus of creating yummy things to enjoy later that become portals back to that magical moment too.

A Time to Prepare

This is a time to preserve the light. A glut of summer fruit preserved in cordial tastes like hope on a cold, dark winter day. A jar of chutney made with tomatoes picked on a sunny afternoon can pep up the beigest of winter comfort food, capturing the light of the sun in every mouthful. A garland made from preserved autumn leaves holds their vivid colour a while longer, ready for when we need it the most. Dried flowers capture the season's beauty. The scent of homemade rosewater distils the essence of summer for when it feels furthest away from us. All glimmers to notice in the moment, but also ones that will keep us going through the darker half.

Our ancestors held this knowledge about the importance of preparation too. It's why the harvest seasons were such a significant part of the rhythm of the year – and not just for practical reasons, storing and preserving food for humans and livestock to keep communities going throughout the winter months. Celebrating harvest also had a vital psychological function: in a society so closely tied to the land, it marked a moment to pause and give thanks to nature and to one another for the fruits of their joint labours.

With no access to long-range weather reports, complex machinery, refrigeration and other modern conveniences, the agricultural year was organised instead around the solstices and equinoxes and life was very much tied to the land.

Harvest, known as 'Hairst' or 'Har'st' in the Scots language, was a time of gratitude for nature's bounty, for gathering together and for preserving and preparing for the winter months, or 'nychtin' time'. While we often think of the equinox as the start of autumn, in the Celtic calendar the harvest seasons began earlier with Lùnastal on 1 August – the rough midpoint between the summer solstice and the September Equinox – as the most abundant period in the seasonal cycle, with crops such as oats, barley and corn golden and swaying in the fields. It finished with Samhain at the end of October and the final harvests and preparation of the land for next year's sowing.

As with many harvest traditions across communities and cultures, generosity, reciprocity and community are key parts of traditional Celtic harvest celebrations. While this sense of interconnectedness has, in many ways, been lost over time in our fast-paced modern world, we can learn a lot from our ancestors whose connection to the land, to the rhythm of the seasons and to one another, created an inter-dependence that ensured community survival. As well as dancing, music and frivolity, there were more serious rituals: 'lovedarg' where people helped their neighbours, the lighting of symbolic bonfires, and superstitious rituals such as the cutting of 'the last sheaf' (see pages 28–29) took place, reinforcing the honouring of the land and strengthening of community bonds as the farming year drew to a close.

Holding Duality

As we head into the unknown and bid goodbye to the summer, this time can often be filled with a mixture of contradictory emotions, anticipation and anxiety co-existing side by side. As August began a few years ago, I felt this jumble of feelings more keenly than ever. I had been doing my own preparations for pregnancy. My partner and I had been trying for a baby for some time, and that year, around Lùnastal, we thought I was pregnant. I'd had so many of the signs we had read about, and my excitement grew with every day my period was late. We were waiting for the advised two weeks to pass before taking a test, neither of us wanting to wed ourselves to the idea too soon, both of us having family in the medical field and knowing the risks of an early loss. It didn't stop me secretly getting excited, holding my breath for the day we could take a test. I had a stash of them ready to go.

Sadly, on the morning of a family wedding I began to bleed. The feeling of loss was profound. I applied my make-up and put on a long dress I could hide in, slapped on a smile and we set off for the venue in Fife.

The rain fell in apocalyptic sheets as we climbed a hill to the small chapel in the East Neuk, the golden fields soggy, the fertile land overcome by late summer storms. I threw confetti and congratulated the happy couple but felt completely hollow inside. I made small talk and grimaced through the 'you'll be next!' comments; I danced a ceilidh in the village hall. But every cramp was a reminder of what we were losing.

How many of us, in times of outward abundance, joy and beauty are masking our inner pain? How many of us hold secrets like the one I did? How many are subject to these kinds of comments and have to smile, politely laugh and change the subject while we are dying inside?

Through it all, the weather matched my mood. Outer storm, inner storm. You just wouldn't write such obvious pathetic fallacy. It was one of those August deluges that herald a shift in the season, that reminds you of the growing and inevitable darkness on the horizon. A shiver, a wake-up, a sign that winter is not far off.

And yet, for all the 'you'll be next' comments, I did have something to hold onto that brought me great solace. Ironically, we had been planning our own wedding in secret – we were eloping to Highland Perthshire the very next month. I swallowed my sadness and channelled my energies into planning the final details of our day.

As I still quietly grieved what was not to be, on 2 September we were married by the waterfall in a forest of Douglas Fir trees near Dunkeld. It was our fifteenth anniversary, and we were accompanied by just two witnesses (our florist and photographer) and our celebrant. We read our vows to each other over an oathing stone, an ancient Celtic tradition whereby tribes would set their promises in stone (thought to be the origin of the saying) connecting important vows – especially wedding vows – to the land and to their ancestors.

I wore an olive green ditsy floral maxi dress and a dried flower crown made with honesty seed heads. My new husband wore a tweed suit in forest green and his best shoes. I carried a bouquet of my favourite blooms and berries: dahlias, cosmos, brambles and rosehips. My husband took photos on his Dad's old film camera. We had a picnic of cardamom buns from Aran Bakery and elderflower champagne from Perthshire by the burn (small stream). It was the most beautiful, aligned and intimate day I have ever experienced: a true celebration of us, and of the harvest season that I will forever associate with a sense of deep fulfilment.

We're not the only ones either – one of the Lùnastal traditions was the 'marriage fair', a time of courting and matchmaking. There are records of simple marriage rituals frequently occurring by stone circles or standing stones (such as the Stones of Stenness or Stone of Odin in Orkney, as immortalised in Sir Walter Scott's *The Pirate*). It felt like what we were doing was truly ancient.

As well as a time of abundance, love and celebration, there must have been a feeling of trepidation about the long winter ahead for our ancestors. A time of duality. This is a feeling that we may also be aware of today: like the plants that expend the last of their energy swelling their fruits and seeds, we can also feel tired after a busy summer, and ready to rest and retreat for a while – even if we also don't want it to end. To sit with these feelings, to hold the paradoxes as one season ends and another begins, to reap what has been sown and prepare the way for winter is such an important part of the year's rhythm, and our own.

In a society where we can get strawberries in December, it might not be obvious why this time was, and is, so important. Learning to listen and look out for the signs from nature and reconnecting with traditional rituals and preparations of the harvest season are ways to head mindfully into the winter to come. A slow letting go of the summer with gratitude and grace, revelling in that golden light and maybe capturing a little too. For we are wavering on the edge of the season's turn, being beckoned gradually into winter's dark cocoon.

'As well as a time of
abundance, love
& celebration,
there must have been
a feeling of
trepidation about the long
winter ahead for
our ancestors.'

Stories from Folklore

When you think about it, it makes a lot of sense that harvest traditions were such pivotal times in the Celtic calendar: in a world where your very existence was so closely tied to the land, taking time to honour nature's bounty, to give thanks for a good harvest and to celebrate with the community as the busiest time of the farming year reached its peak must have seemed the most natural thing in the world. Each and every grain that was harvested was a genuine cause for celebration, since it meant your chances of surviving winter increased. It was also a release after the hard work of tending the harvest from seed to crop in preparation for the darker half of the year. This is an approach that we could all take inspiration from: to give ourselves permission to down our tools a while, even when life is at its busiest; to pause and give thanks to nature for all that it gives us.

In Scotland, there were different names for harvest celebrations in different places, but the first and most famous of the traditional Gaelic celebrations associated with Hairst began with Lùnastal (in Scottish Gaelic), also known as Lughnasadh (in Irish Gaelic) and related to Lammas (from the Anglo-Saxon 'hlafmaesse', meaning loaf feast). There are many theories as to the origins of the festival, but its timing around 1 August dates back many thousands of years according to the Coligny calendar, a Celtic calendar from the Roman period found in France in the nineteenth century.

Most theories associate Lùnastal with the Celtic god of the sun, light and harvest, Lugh, who is especially important in Ireland. Surviving folklore tells of the deity's prowess as a warrior and his triumph over the underworld, the god Crom Dubh (or Crom Cruach), who tried to keep the grain for himself. Lugh eventually won back the grain for humanity, the fight represented in stories as being over a woman called Eithne who symbolises the grain. In later folklore, the story was Christianised with Lugh replaced by Saint Patrick, who converted Crom Dubh to Christianity. In other stories linked to harvest, Lugh has to fight the evil giant Balor in order to overcome drought and disease and bring successful harvest for humankind.

Lughnasadh is often associated with hill climbing, games and contests, as Lugh is thought to have founded the ancient Tailteann Games to honour his foster-mother Tailtiu who was said to have cleared the land in preparation for farming and subsequently died of exhaustion. The Games, held in the last two weeks of July and culminating with Lughnasadh, included mourning ceremonies, the proclamation of new laws and handfastings, and competitions for entertainment, including the long jump, running, archery, sword fighting, horse racing and more. A god of many talents, Lugh was also the deity of arts, skills and crafts, meaning there were competitions for singing, dancing, storytelling and artisan crafts such as jewellery and weaving.

The original Games took place where Tailtiu was buried, Teltown in Country Meath, Ireland, but the festivities soon spread and were brought across the Irish Sea to become part of harvest celebrations in Scotland too. Lammas Fairs were held across the country and would often include a Harvest Home feast, where the whole community spent time together sharing the fruits of their labour, with the freshly harvested food and drink plentiful. It was a thank you for all involved. Baking bread from the year's harvest such as the struan loaf (see page 51) was an important tradition, symbolic of community harmony. Later, in Christianised communities, harvest festivals became incorporated into the Christian feast of Michaelmas on 29 September.

During harvest, there would be offerings made to the gods and to nature itself, to thank the land and its deities for – hopefully – a successful harvest and to keep evil spirits at bay. The first fruits of the harvest were offered up to the gods and bulls were sacrificed in the Scottish Highlands. There are records of cattle 'saining' or blessings, live animals' tails and ears being tarred or decorated with blue and red threads. In the Highlands, folk made 'lunastain' cakes, a type of bannock or flatbread made with oats, thought to be another form of offering. Bonfires would also be lit, symbolic of protection and seen as purifying the land.

As well as an annual marker of thanksgiving and the filling up of the winter stores, harvest was an important part of consolidating wider community identity, a reflection on the summer gone and a way of strengthening bonds for the winter ahead. Workers would seek new employment at 'feeing markets' but there was also a strong tradition of community giving. The Gaelic word 'lovedarg' translates as 'work done for love', whereby members of the community would help neighbours – especially those new to the area, ill or otherwise finding working the land challenging – without the expectation of payment. The harvest celebrations themselves became their own kind of payment for this communal work and increased the sense of community – kindness and mutual favours between neighbours would be essential to prepare for and survive the darker months.

Storytelling and reflection were part of many of the seasonal festivals in the Celtic cycle, and this was true during harvest celebrations as well. One example is the cutting of 'the last sheaf', or 'sguab mu dheireadh' in Scottish Gaelic, our version of the superstition existing throughout Northern Europe. There are different traditions relating to 'the last sheaf' across Scotland, but generally rural folks believed that within the grain was a Spirit of the Harvest who would move from grain to grain as they were cut down by hand and would remain in the last grain to be cut, its magic becoming more and more concentrated as it passed from field to field.

The spirit was known by different names and was called the 'maighdean-bhuana' (harvest maiden) or the 'cailleach-bhuaineadh' (old woman of the harvest), goddess of winter or earth mother. The last grain of the first field to be harvested (usually wheat, oats or barley) would be made into a Cailleach doll (sometimes a woven corn dolly dressed in wee clothes, or sometimes just a plait or knot of grain decorated with a ribbon or flowers) that was then passed onto the next farmer's field, then the next, and so on. This continued until the doll reached the last farm in the vicinity to complete the harvest. The cutting of the last sheaf was sometimes done by the youngest girl in the community, or the oldest woman.

Many communities were superstitious of the doll, so nobody wanted to be the last farm to harvest their grain, because they didn't want to have to care for the Cailleach doll during the winter months. That said, in other places, the doll was thought to bring good luck and was displayed in the house through wintertime, memorialising the success of the harvest. The tradition created a feeling of competition, ensuring the crop was secured quickly and safely before the weather turned. When Imbolc eventually arrived, marking the start of the lighter months, the doll was ploughed back into the fields or fed to livestock for good luck in the season ahead.

'During harvest,

there would be offerings

made to the gods

and to nature itself.'

Finding Light

Harvest Flowers

August and September, and even early October – or at least until the first frosts – offer a flurry of late summer and early autumn flowers, the crescendo of the growing season. September, with one foot in summer and the other in autumn, will always be a favourite time of mine for flowers – and not just because it contains both my birthday and anniversary! There's a quiet magic to this month of glorious transitions, as the last of the season's blooms cross paths with the first changing leaves, hips and berries. A moment to be savoured and preserved before the descent into winter.

As well as the important harvest gathering of oats, wheat and grains to provide staple foods throughout the dormant seasons, the community gathering of our ancestors would also have included the stockpiling of resources for making fires (such as flammable gorse and bracken for kindling) and herbal and medicinal ingredients – that is, plants, including their flowers, roots and seeds – as the growing seasons came to an end.

As well as the edible makes that I will mention in this chapter using the flowers and fruits of early autumn, it has become a kind of tradition of my own to pick and preserve the last of the flowers from my teeny pot garden for crafting purposes too; after all, we need to harvest beauty to sustain us through the winter months as well. So here are some autumn flowers to savour, all at their peak in the harvest seasons and perfect for adorning celebratory tables and autumnal arrangements. While most of these are non-native and certainly not ancient Scottish flowers, this list is reflective of the flowers that gardeners, growers and the network of local flower farmers are celebrating in the UK today.

Dahlias

If there was one flower that summed up this time in the growing season for me, it would be the dahlia. They come in all shapes and sizes, from dinner-plate-sized blooms with ruffled petals to pom-pom spheres to skinny starburst ones. I like their predominantly warm palette, and how prolific they are: the more you cut, the more they come (just make sure the flowers have opened before you pick them or they won't unfurl). Remember that they are native to Mexico and Central America, so if you're growing them make sure they have a warm, sunny spot and don't over-water them.

Cosmos

Cosmos flowers are almost cartoonish with their delicate, daisy-like petals. Again, their warm colour palette seems suited to the harvest seasons but they flower all summer long too. They also like full sun and don't like soggy feet. My favourite is the chocolate cosmos, with its small, deep burgundy red, almost brown velvety petals that even smell curiously chocolatey – they contain the compound vanillin, which is also in cocoa. They are also cut-and-come-again flowers, so cut more to encourage them to flower from mid-spring to the end of autumn.

Chrysanthemums

As a cut flower, chrysanthemums have great longevity in the vase and come in shades from deep red all the way through to white. They need warmth and light and plenty of water. You can get all sorts of types from large globe-like blooms to smaller ditsy versions. They symbolise longevity, joy and optimism but are also associated with mourning.

Asters

Asters are also known as Michaelmas daisies because of when they bloom in late summer and early autumn. The best-known version of the flower has purple blooms, and they are often found wild in sunny, well-drained areas. The name 'aster' comes from the ancient Greek for 'star', an apt reflection of their shape. As the September birth flower they are thought to represent patience, love and wisdom.

Rudbeckias

The flowers of rudbeckia are most well-known in their palette of bee-like yellow petals with black cone centres, but those grown as annuals also come in dark reds, dusky oranges and earthy browns. They love sun and look beautiful in prairie-style gardens along with ornamental grasses. The distinctive seedheads of the rudbeckia persist well into the winter if you leave them, providing seeds for the birds.

Drying Dahlias

When we eloped in the September of2023, one of our witnesses was our friend and florist Marion, who made me the most beautiful, locally grown bouquet with the textures and flowers of early autumn as though gathered from the garden and foraged from the hedgerow: dahlias in café au lait, peach and deep wine, rust-coloured rudbeckias, chocolate cosmos, burgundy ammi, fragrant blush-pink sweet peas, buttery phlox and dusky-pink roses. Interspersed throughout the bouquet were blackberries and rosehips, elder, bracken and honesty seed pods in a beautifully wild summer-meets-autumn arrangement.

When we got home, I dried out some of the dahlias from the bouquet and will treasure their wiggly dried petals forever. They are surprisingly easy to preserve and have their own sculptural appeal that lends itself to wreath making – so make them now and save them for the coming season as a reminder of long, sunny days when you need it.

You will need:
Dahlia flowers
Scissors
Twine
Toilet-roll or kitchen-roll tubes

Wait until the very end of the season, when the plants have almost stopped producing more blooms, before cutting your dahlia flowers.

Leave the stem long, that way you can cut it shorter depending on what you want to use them for later.

For the pom-pom variety, cut a length of twine long enough for you to tie several stems together without the flower heads touching. Dry your dahlias by tying a loop and suspending them upside down from the ceiling in a well-ventilated area. If you can, make sure it is out of direct sunlight to prevent their colour from fading.

For varieties that have more of a star-like or spidery shape, it is best to dry them upright to stop the flowers curling up and losing their distinctive forms. Prop them up in toilet-roll or kitchen-roll tubes, and leave them somewhere out of the light and with plenty of air to circulate.

Tip

— Alternatively, you can dry dahlias by leaving them in a little water until they start to shrink, then remove them from the water and use one of the options above to complete the drying process. The finish will be more rustic, but no less beautiful.

Rosewater

The smell of roses has got to be one of the most evocative of the summer months; just a drop of the scent in the depths of winter can transport you back to those sunnier memories. Rosewater originated in Persia (modern day Iran) and is used as perfume in beauty products and is thought to reduce redness and soothe and moisturise the skin. You can also make your own potpourri by mixing rosewater with dried rose petals, lavender or herbs in a jar, making sure the dried flowers are saturated before drying them out and topping them up with a few drops as necessary.

Rosewater can also be used in cookery, especially sweet treats such as Turkish delight. There are several different ways to make rosewater, including distilling (for a concentrated rosewater using a more involved process) and simmering (for a less potent rosewater but a very easy method, which I include here). It's important to make sure any roses that you use haven't been sprayed with chemicals or pesticides – try to get organic ones if you can. If you don't grow your own, you can ask your local flower farmer or florist to source some for you.

Makes approx. 200ml
3 rose flowers
A large saucepan
300ml distilled (or boiled and cooled) water
Strainer
Glass jar

Prepare your fresh petals: remove them from the flowers by pulling them gently away from the stem and pop them into the saucepan.

Add enough water to just cover the petals – you may not need the whole amount listed (too much will dilute the rosewater).

Place the pan on a low heat, cover with a lid and let the water slowly come to the boil. Leave it to simmer gently until the petals lose their colour – around 30 minutes.

Leave the liquid (now your rosewater!) to cool, then strain it into a jar and refrigerate it until you want to use it.

Rosehip Syrup

Rosehips contain abundant vitamin C: during World War II, with citrus in short supply, the Ministry of Food advised citizens to collect rosehips to make into syrup as a local alternative to imported citrus fruit – rosehips have as much as twenty times the amount of vitamin C as the equivalent weight of oranges. It was even given to babies for many years after the war (just don't mention the sugar) and thus a generation was raised on this hedgerow syrup. Further still into the past, archaeological digs have found that rosehips have been eaten for thousands of years – thought to be protective and to treat digestive issues.

In Scotland, rosehips are known as 'itchy coos' (cows) because of the small, irritating hairs found within – children would prank one another by putting them down the neck of each other's clothes to make them itch. As such, it's important to remove the fine hairs before you consume them! Rosehips have a naturally sweet-sharp flavour and an almost appley taste – apt, because apples are actually part of the rose family. Rosehips can be frozen or dried once picked to preserve them, but remember to leave plenty for the birds as they are an important source of food in the winter.

Makes approx. 200ml
500g rosehips
500ml water
Caster sugar, as needed

Start by prepping your rosehips: give them a good wash to remove any beasties.

Using a food processor, roughly chop the rosehips, then pop them into a large pan, cover with 500ml of water and place over a medium heat.

Bring the mixture to the boil and simmer for 15–20 minutes.

Line a sieve with two layers of muslin and pour the mixture through. Leave it to strain for at least 30 minutes – you want to extract as much juice as you can.

Repeat the straining process with clean muslin to make sure any fine hairs are completely removed.

Meanwhile, sterilise a 250ml bottle by washing it in hot, soapy water, rinsing it well and leaving it to dry out in the oven at 110°C/Fan 100°C/Gas Mark ¼.

Measure the rosehip juice into a large saucepan. For every 100ml juice, you want to add 60g sugar.

Place the pan over a low heat, stirring regularly and making sure that the sugar has dissolved before you bring the mixture to the boil.

Raise the heat to bring the mixture to the boil and cook for around 5 minutes. If a frothy scum forms on the surface, remove it with a spoon.

Pour the mixture into your prepared bottle while it is still warm from sterilising in the oven, and seal straight away.

Tips

- Use the syrup as you would maple syrup – it is lovely on pancakes or drizzled on your porridge.
- Make sure you use the syrup within a few months, and store it in the fridge once the bottle has been opened. Alternatively, you can store it in portions in an ice cube tray in the freezer.

Traffic Light Tomato Chutney

For many summers, too many of my tomatoes, lovingly tended over the warmer months, have failed to ripen and stay stubbornly green on the plant. While they can still be ripening into October here, sometimes there's simply not enough sunlight and too much rain before the frosts arrive. While you can ripen them up in a brown paper bag with a banana (the ethylene emitted by bananas encourages them to ripen) they're sometimes not the tastiest or the biggest, and need their flavour coaxed out with cooking. To avoid food waste, I came up with my traffic light tomato chutney – so called because it makes the most of multicoloured tomatoes, including green ones! Use what you have and adapt to your own tastes.

Makes 2 x 350ml jars

500g tomatoes (a mixture of any colour)
100g onion, finely chopped
100g sultanas
1 apple, cored and chopped (keep the skin on)
1 tbsp fennel seeds
1 tbsp coriander seeds
75g soft brown sugar
400ml cider vinegar

Mix all the ingredients together in a large, heavy-bottomed pan.

Place on the hob over a medium heat until the sugar dissolves in the vinegar.

Raise the heat and bring to a boil, then turn it down to a simmer. Leave on the hob without a lid to quietly simmer for up to 3 hours, stirring occasionally, until the fruit and vegetables have all cooked and the mixture has reduced.

Sterilise your jars by washing them with warm, soapy water then drying them in the oven at 110°C/Fan 100°C/Gas Mark ¼. Boil the lids in a pan of water to sterilise them too.

Once the chutney is ready and while it is still warm, decant into the still-warm sterilised jars and seal with the lids.

Tip

— The chutney will keep for around 12 months in a cool, dark place. The flavours will mingle and develop deliciously. Once opened, store it in the fridge where it will last for a few weeks.

Strawberry Top Cordial

I'm always looking for ways to use up kitchen scraps rather than putting them in the compost bin – whether that's freezing vegetable peel to save for making stock, or making orange peel into citrus cleaning spray (see page 183). I found myself looking at strawberry tops – the fuzzy green stars that joined them to the plant, and the inevitable bit of fruit that hangs onto them when you top and hull the strawberry – and wondering if there was something I could do with them. You can actually eat the green bits, popping them into smoothies or infusing water with them, but I thought I'd go a step further to distil their essence for the darker months and came up with this strawberry top cordial, which tastes like a greener version of strawberries. I collect the tops from a couple of punnets in a bag in the freezer to keep them fresh, then follow the steps below. Delicious served diluted with soda water and a handful of crushed mint leaves.

Makes 1 x 400ml bottle

2 x 250g punnet's worth of strawberry tops, frozen
250ml water
250g caster sugar

Add the strawberry tops and water to a large saucepan along with the caster sugar and heat gently over a low heat to dissolve the sugar.

Raise the temperature to bring the mixture to the boil, then turn down the heat and simmer for around 15 minutes until it has the consistency of a light syrup (it will thicken further as it cools).

Remove the saucepan from the heat and set aside to let the strawberry top cordial infuse overnight.

The next day, sterilise your bottle by washing it in warm water and popping it in the oven at 110°C/Fan 100°C/Gas Mark ¼ to dry completely. Sterilise any metal stoppers in a pan of boiling water.

Strain your cordial into a jug then pour into the sterilised bottle.

Tip

– The cordial will keep for a month or so in a cool, dark place, and make sure you store it in the fridge once opened. To store the cordial for longer, freeze it in an ice cube tray and defrost a cube at a time as needed.

Autumn Leaf Guide

Here in Scotland, the leaves on the trees usually begin to turn in late August and early September, their dramatic colour peaking in mid- to late-October. The transformation from green to crimson, gold, russet and orange is one of the surest signs of autumn's arrival. This change is brought about by a drop in temperature combined with shorter days: with less light, trees stop producing the chlorophyll that makes their leaves green and converts light into energy to grow – revealing the red and yellow pigments (anthocyanins and carotenes respectively). A combination of cold weather, bright sunshine and dry spells leads to the most spectacular displays of autumn colour before the trees lose their leaves. The subsequent leaf fall enables trees to preserve precious moisture during the winter and become dormant to conserve energy and survive the cold and stormy weather.

Horse Chestnut

Aesculus hippocastanum

The horse chestnut is usually one of the first trees to turn, heralding the end of summer and start of autumn with its leaves transforming into shades of scarlet and ochre in contrast with its vivid green, spiky shells containing their mahogany hued conkers. Their leaves are palmate, with five to seven leaves fanning out from their central stem. They tend to fall soon after turning yellow, and rapidly turn to mush in the autumn rain. Mature chestnut trees can grow up to forty metres tall.

Aspen

Populus tremula

The aspen was named *Populus tremula* because of its trembling leaves, and it is also referred to often as the 'quaking aspen' due to the light movement of its leaves. In Celtic superstition, this shimmering was thought to represent communication between the worlds of the living and the dead. Its leaves are round with irregular, slightly rounded teeth. The aspen's new growth is almost copper in colour, and they turn a vivid yellow or sometimes an orangey red in the autumn. It is most common in the UK in north-west Scotland.

Rowan
Sorbus aucuparia
The rowan tree is also important in Celtic folklore, as it was thought to protect against evil, including witches, and was often planted near homes. In fact, it was seen as unthinkable to cut one down in Scotland. The rowan thrives in high altitudes and is prolific in the wilds, especially the Highlands. Its leaves are formed of five to eight pairs of opposite oval, toothed leaflets with a further leaflet on the end. Once pollinated, its summer flowers transform into scarlet berries – at one time thought to be magical – that are popular with birds who disperse their seeds in turn. Its leaves turn yellow, orange and red in the early autumn.

Hazel
Corylus avellana
The hazel has oval, pointed leaves that turn yellow before they fall in the autumn. Once pollinated, the female flowers form oval fruits that ripen into nuts, which are encased in cups of leafy bracts containing clusters of between one and four nuts. In late winter and early spring, the hazel's main identifying feature is its male flowers before the leaves come out – long strings of yellow catkins that appear in mid-February. The hazel was also known as a magical tree, offering protection against the spirit world (especially if you held a hazel rod or wand) and representing wisdom and inspiration.

Oak

Quercus robur

The common oak is typically one of the later trees to lose its distinctive lobed, smooth leaves, which grow in bundles and turn a beautiful golden brown. Oaks produce acorns that turn from green to brown as they ripen and fall to the ground ready to sprout next spring. In Celtic mythology the oak is thought to be sacred and was referred to as the 'King of the Forest', representing strength.

Beech

Fagus sylvatica

The beech tree is often known as the Queen of British trees to the Oak's King and is symbolic of femininity. Fagus was God of beech trees in Celtic mythology and the beech was believed to symbolise wisdom and to have healing properties. Their leaves have a distinctive oval shape and wavy edge, and, depending on the variety, turn shades of golden brown through to copper. They are distinctive as a 'marcescent' type of tree, meaning that on many (but not all) trees, the leaves turn brown but remain on the tree throughout wintertime, especially on the lower branches and in hedgerow varieties, protecting new growth and only falling when the fresh buds arrive in the spring. In the autumn they also produce beech masts – small, triangular nuts encased in burrs that open into star-shaped cases that can be seen in great numbers upon the forest floor.

Sycamore

Acer pseudoplatanus

The sycamore is a broadleaf tree that is native to Europe and can live for up to 400 years. Its bark has a pinkish hue, and its leaves have five lobes, turning orange and red in October. Its winged seeds are often referred to as 'helicopters', used in flying competitions by children. The sycamore is revered across cultures as a symbol of strength and endurance; it is a sacred tree in Celtic folklore, thought to connect heaven, earth and the underworld. People believed it was home to fairies and it was often planted near the home as a symbolic form of protection.

Silver Birch

Betula pendula

The birch has small, serrated leaves transforming into vivid yellow hues before falling like rain in their myriads in late October and November. In the spring the birch has downy yellow catkins, known colloquially as lambs' tails. In Celtic mythology, the birch was thought to symbolise renewal, cleansing and protection as well as love and fertility. Its twigs were used for a variety of purposes – as brooms to sweep away the old year (literally and metaphorically) and as a fertility charm for livestock; in Highland folklore it was believed that cows herded with birch sticks would become pregnant and carry healthy calves.

'The transformation
from green to
crimson, gold, russet
& orange is one
of the surest signs
of autumn's arrival.'

Beeswax Everlasting Leaves

The soft autumn light, filtered through a canopy of golden and ruby red leaves has got to be one of the most beautiful seasonal sights, an annual reminder of nature's beauty but also its transience. And while I aim to be present and savour the moment above all, part of me always wants to capture a little of the spirit of the autumn and preserve that gorgeous light and colour a little longer. These everlasting leaves are dipped in beeswax in order to do so, a preserving medium that has been used for thousands of years.

Traces of beeswax have been found in ancient Celtic pottery, where it was thought to preserve and even sweeten drinks and was used to seal containers. It was also found in tombs, so may have had a ritualistic, spiritual dimension too. You can make your everlasting leaves into a garland by tying or pegging the beeswax dipped leaves onto a piece of twine. Arrange the leaves on a flat surface first in the order you want – think about the colours, sizes and shapes and alternate them for balance.

You will need:

- Autumn leaves – distinctive shapes such as sycamore, Japanese maple and oak leaves work well
- A damp cloth
- Kitchen roll or a tea towel, for drying the leaves
- A stack of heavy books
- A shallow heatproof dish, such as a medium-sized Pyrex dish, that can fit inside one of your pans. Make sure you don't mind using it for other waxy crafts as it will be difficult to clean!

First, prepare your leaves – you want to make sure they're clean with no dirt on them to ensure the beeswax has a flat, even surface to cling to. Either wipe with a damp cloth or give them a rinse under the tap and dry thoroughly.

Place your leaves in a single layer between sheets of kitchen roll, then pop them underneath a stack of heavy books to press them flat. Leave for at least a few days to flatten. You can skip this step if you want but the results will be better if you can take the time.

When you're ready to preserve your leaves, measure your beeswax into the heatproof dish. Add a few centimetres of water to the saucepan, making sure it isn't so deep that it will overflow into your dish when you add it, and bring the water to a simmer.

Place your heatproof dish with the beeswax inside carefully into the water and stir occasionally while the beeswax melts and becomes clear with no cloudy bits.

100–200g beeswax pellets (the amount depends on the size of your heatproof dish: you need enough to be able to submerge the leaves fully.
A large saucepan
A spoon or palette knife to stir with (again, that you don't mind getting waxy)
A baking sheet
Baking parchment

Meanwhile, prep your baking sheet with parchment on top, ready to receive the leaves.

Using the stem to dip them, take one leaf at a time and submerge it fully in the beeswax, ensuring it coats both sides for a few seconds.

Lift the leaf out using the stem and leave it to drip for a few seconds over the heatproof dish – it's important you remove as much excess beeswax as possible for a smooth finish on the back so don't rush this step. Once you have done this, transfer the leaf to the prepared baking sheet, laying it face up.

The leaves will begin to set almost immediately. If you notice there is excess wax on parts of the leaf, you can dip again, holding it in the wax for a little longer so that the first coat of wax melts into the mixture and your leaf is re-coated, then leave to drip for a little longer to remove more excess than previously.

Repeat for all your leaves, setting them aside on the tray to cool. Use as desired!

If you have leftover wax, you can pour this into a silicone ice cube tray to re-use it for other projects, such as beeswax candles (see page 94) or wraps.

Tip

— If you are using the preserved leaves for a craft where you will see both sides, you could try pegging them onto a piece of string above a baking tray lined with parchment to catch any drips for a smoother result on both back and front.

Embracing Darkness

Harvest Fermentation

Fermentation is one of the oldest methods of preserving; although it's recently been a trend in the food and wellness world, it has actually been around for thousands of years. Fermenting is a way of using natural yeasts and bacteria to break down the carbohydrates in food and preserve it, which was vital in times before refrigeration. The ancient Celts used honey for fermentation and preservation purposes, especially in mead – a fermented honey drink.

The process of fermentation results in unique, tangy flavours and is now known to have benefits for our gut health, as fermented foods are easier for us to digest too. Fermentation is best done in the dark (well, storing your ferments in the dark while the bacteria do their job!) as light can inhibit the fermentation process by slowing the growth and activity of yeast and bacteria, and possibly leading to spoilage. Store your ferments in a cool, dark place such as a cupboard.

Of course, fermented oats would have to be Scotland's national ferment! Because of the country's cold and wet climate, oats – rather than wheat – were the main crop and a staple part of the diet. Sowans (pronounced 'soo-an') were a dish made from the discarded oat husks and they taste a bit like the sour flavour of milk kefir. Most households would have a 'sowan bowie' – a small barrel-like tub – where they made sowans. It would be filled with oat husks or 'sids', warm water and salt. The solids would be pressed below the surface of the water and the whole thing left to ferment. After a week or so, the mixture would be sieved before being left for a further couple of days to settle into a yellowy liquid (the 'swats' – a clear drink) and a white paste below (the sowans).

The process of making sowans is what we would now call lacto-fermenting, which is making a fermented foodstuff by adding salt, either in the form of a brine, or by salting the ingredients sufficiently so that they release their own water and create a salt solution. Sowans were used in numerous ways: reduced down into a thick cream, enriched with butter, cooked like a porridge or used as an ingredient in baking in the manner of buttermilk.

These days, during harvest season I'm inclined to use fermentation techniques to preserve the late summer and early autumn gluts of fruit and vegetables to see me through the darker half of the year. I've used plums in the recipe overleaf as they work beautifully with the honey, but you could adapt this for any summer fruit. The fermented fruit is delicious anywhere you would use a compote, such as on porridge or yoghurt for breakfast. A few summers ago, I attended a workshop with River Cottage's Rachel de Thample at Bowhouse, Fife, as part of the Spots on My Apples Festival. There, she taught us the honey-fermentation method and we distilled the flavours of the East Neuk into jars to enjoy for many months to come. I've had the bug ever since – it's such a lovely way to capture seasonal flavours, especially in the busy harvest season, when you might not want to be standing over a hot stove to make jam.

Spiced Honey-fermented Plums

Plums and honey taste gorgeous together, and both sing of the harvest season. Adding star anise brings a lovely warmly spiced, aromatic note – but you could leave it out if you're not a fan. Time is the main ingredient here, turning your honeyed plums into a deliciously pickled sweet and tangy ferment. You can use this method with other fruits, and it works really quickly with soft summer berries (as their juices help to start the fermentation process). If you are using stone fruit, chop it into chunks for a faster ferment like I do here.

Makes 1 x 350ml jar (but you can easily scale this up or down)

2 large plums (around 200–250g), stones removed
2 whole star anise (optional)
300g runny honey, or enough to cover the plums and fill the jar (raw, local honey has the best health benefits, so use this if you can)

Sterilise your jar by washing it in warm water, then drying it in the oven at 110°C/Fan 100°C/Gas Mark ¼. Allow to cool.

Chop your plums into 2cm chunks and fill the jar with them up to about two thirds full.

Add your star anise, if using.

Cover the plums with honey, allowing it to settle around the fruit then adding more if necessary to fill the jar up to the top, then seal it.

Leave the jar to ferment at room temperature in a cool, dark place for at least a week. Every other day, release some air by loosening the lid slightly to 'burp' your ferment before sealing tightly. Invert the jar to mix the contents regularly too.

Tips

— Make sure there's a plate underneath your fermenting jar as you store it, in case of leaks as the fermentation gets going.
— Discard your ferment if you find any mould on the surface, which means the vessel has become contaminated. Fermentation uses bacteria, but the friendly bacteria naturally occurring in the fruit – any others can be harmful.

Easy Apple and Fennel Seed Bread

The struan loaf was traditionally baked in September around Michaelmas and was a cross between a scone and a pancake, cooked on the griddle. It used to be made with ewe's milk, then later buttermilk – a by-product of butter making – which was cheaper than cow's milk and kept better in a time before refrigeration. Buttermilk also has a beautiful tenderising effect and tangy flavour and contributes to a good rise when used in combination with bicarbonate of soda (similar to an Irish soda bread). The struan cake was usually flavoured with dried fruit and warming spices such as caraway. Here, I have used yoghurt and milk as a substitute for buttermilk, replaced the dried fruit with fresh apple and added fennel for its warming aniseed flavour.

Makes 1 loaf

- 200g plain flour, plus extra for dusting
- 100g plain white spelt flour
- 1 tsp bicarbonate of soda
- ½ tsp salt
- 2 tsp fennel seeds, plus more for sprinkling
- 2 small apples, chopped into roughly 1cm pieces
- 200g plain yoghurt
- 100g whole milk

Preheat the oven to 200°C/Fan 180°C/Gas Mark 6. Put a baking tray in to warm.

Mix the flours, bicarbonate of soda, salt and fennel seeds with a wooden spoon in a large mixing bowl. Add the chopped apples and stir.

Mix the yoghurt and milk in a separate jug, then add to the dry ingredients. Stir until the mixture comes together into a firm, sticky dough.

On a floured surface, bring the dough together lightly with your hands (as though you are making a scone rather than kneading a loaf of bread), patting it into a round approx. 20cm across.

Remove the warmed baking tray from the oven, lightly flour it or place some parchment on top and place the bread on the tray. Using a sharp knife, score a deep cross in the top of the bread and sprinkle with more fennel seeds.

Bake for 40 minutes, until browned, and when you tip it upside down and tap on the bottom it sounds hollow.

Leave to cool on a wire rack, then cut into slices and serve slathered with salted butter.

Tip

— This bread is best eaten fresh on the day that you make it, but it also freezes well in slices – defrost and toast for best results.

End of Summerfruit Mascarpone Cake

This summerfruit cake made with mascarpone is rich and puddingy, and simply shows off the best of the end of the season's ingredients, making it perfect for harvest celebrations. The addition of mascarpone makes for a tender crumb and sweeter note that balances the sharpness from the fruit beautifully. You can use the rest of the tub of mascarpone to make a sweet, vanilla-scented mascarpone cream to serve alongside the cake. Make the cake earlier in the harvest season with strawberries or later on with blackberries, or a mixture of berries is lovely too. This recipe also works beautifully with cherries, which are in season earlier in the summer.

Serves 8

For the cake:
30g butter, softened
120g caster sugar
90g mascarpone
2 large, free-range eggs
120g self-raising flour
120g summerfruit of your choosing, prepared and chopped into 1cm chunks
60g summerfruit jam of your choosing

For the whipped mascarpone cream:
160g mascarpone
1 tbsp maple syrup
1 tsp vanilla extract

Preheat the oven to 160°C/140°C Fan/Gas Mark 3 and grease and line a round 20cm tin. Using a stand mixer or a bowl and wooden spoon, cream the butter and sugar together until combined.

Add the mascarpone and mix again until the mixture is smooth with no lumps.

Add the eggs to the mixture one at a time with a little flour, beating briefly until fully incorporated. Fold in the rest of the flour, then fold the fruit through the mixture.

Pour the mixture into the prepared tin and smooth the surface with a spatula. Dollop some jam on top and swirl it around with a spoon. If your jam has a firm set, you can warm it a little in a small pan or in short bursts in the microwave to make this easier.

Bake for 30–35 minutes until golden brown and a skewer inserted in the middle comes out clean. Set aside to cool a little in the tin, then turn out onto a wire rack to cool completely.

Meanwhile, make the mascarpone topping. In a large bowl, whisk the mascarpone together with the maple syrup and vanilla extract – be careful not to over mix or the mascarpone will curdle.

Serve in slices with a spoonful of the mascarpone topping on each.

Tip

— For a taste of this cake's summer indulgence in the depths of winter, you can use frozen fruit instead – just add 5–10 minutes to the bake time.

Clay Pressed Botanical Imprints

As well as the sights, scents and colours of late summer and early autumn flowers, their shapes and textures often take on a more structural silhouette that lends itself to a different kind of botanical preserving: clay imprints. I preserved part of my wedding bouquet in this way. Local botanical artist Katy Eccles made an imprint cast from sweetpeas, cosmos and rosehips from my bouquet and it's now a beautiful artwork that hangs in our house to remind us of the day. Inspired by this, I've experimented with using air-dry clay, which is surprisingly simple but incredibly effective. Make sure you use stems, leaves and flowers that have distinctive shapes and aren't too soft for clearest results, such as lavender or small rosebuds. They should be really fresh, or it will be difficult to make a clear impression. You can use the imprints as an art piece or a hanging decoration, or even as gift tags for the festive season.

You will need:
- Air-dry clay
- Cutting mat or chopping board
- Greaseproof paper
- Rolling pin
- Palette knife
- Ruler or cookie cutter
- Knitting needle or skewer, if you want to make a hole and hang your imprint
- A small bowl of warm water
- Flowers (see above)
- A heavy book

Place your air-dry clay on your cutting mat or chopping board with greaseproof paper on top and roll it out into a rectangle approximately 5mm thick. Cut it into your desired shape – you can use a knife and ruler for straight edged squares and rectangles or use a cookie cutter to cut out shapes. If you want to be able to hang your imprint, use a knitting needle to poke a hole in the top.

Soften the edges of the clay by dipping your finger in a little warm water and smoothing any corners or rough bits.

Arrange your flowers on top of the air-dry clay shape. Consider your design: do you want them 'growing up' from the bottom, overlapping or in distinct, separate areas? Press each flower into the clay firmly, leaving a clear impression.

Once you are happy with your impression, carefully remove the flowers before removing the clay from the cutting mat and placing another piece of greaseproof paper on top. Place a heavy book on top – this will stop the clay from curling up at the sides as it dries. Leave to dry completely, as per the air-dry clay's instructions.

Tip

— You can paint your imprints with watercolour paints: start with a pale wash and build up a layer at a time then seal with varnish.

Botanical Printing with Flowers

As the end of summer gives way to autumn's first frosts, it's time to say goodbye to the flower seasons for another year. Botanical printing, also known as bundle dying or eco printing is an easy, eco-friendly way to preserve late summer's floral colours and shapes in fabric at home without any harsh chemicals. The pattern and colour you create will be a beautiful reminder of the floral seasons on winter's barest days.

In botanical printing, steam is used to extract the natural pigments from the materials and, as you're using the plants directly rather than making them into a dye, it also makes a beautiful pattern. It's easier to do than making your own dye for a vat or dye bath and creates a more vivid result. Plus, you can use old household equipment that you already have to hand (I always keep crafting tools separate to kitchen ones). You could use this method to dye old T-shirts to breathe new life into them or revive stained kitchen tea towels. The vinegar helps to set the dye and makes the colours more vivid, but if you don't have any the colours may fade faster but will still be beautiful.

You will need:

- Light-coloured fabric made from natural fibres such as cotton or linen
- Something to protect your surface e.g. an old towel
- White vinegar in a spray bottle
- Flower heads/petals (e.g. cosmos, roses and pansies)
- Thin paper e.g. parchment paper
- String
- Scissors
- Kitchen steamer pot (or you can make one by using a pan with a colander, sieve or steamer basket on top and a lid over)
- Kitchen tongs
- Iron

First, soak your fabric in cold water overnight, or for at least several hours.

Cover your surface with something to protect it. Squeeze out the excess water and lay your fabric flat on the surface.

Spray the fabric all over with the vinegar.

Decorate your fabric: pick off the petals and their middles, arranging them over the surface of the material. Consider your design: do you want the placement to be deliberate or random? Do you want a mixture of bigger and smaller petals? How do you want the different colours to be distributed? Play around with the placement.

When you're happy with your design, spray it with more vinegar.

Place the paper over the top of the design and press it down firmly. Starting at one end, roll the fabric tightly, keeping the paper in the middle. Tie together tightly with string along the length of your rolled fabric, then roll this into a spiral (like a snail shell). Wrap this tightly with more string to secure your bundle.

Add a few centimetres of water to your steamer pot and bring it to the boil. If you are using the colander method, make sure the water isn't touching the bottom of the colander.

Place your bundle into the steamer and place the lid on top.

Leave to steam for 15 minutes, then use the tongs to turn the bundle and steam it for a further 15 minutes. Keep an eye on the water to make sure it doesn't boil dry, and top up if necessary.

Remove the bundle using the tongs and set it aside to cool and for the colour to develop. The longer you leave it before unfurling, the stronger the colour will be – 24 hours is good.

The next day, place the surface protector on your surface again. Remove the string from your bundle and unroll the fabric, then remove the parchment paper.

Gently remove any remaining plants from the fabric using the pads of your fingers to rub them off. Shake the fabric to remove any final pieces of plant material (this is maybe best done outside!).

Leave the fabric to air dry flat, then iron with a hot steam iron to set the dye.

Tips

- If you need to wash your botanically printed fabric, make sure to do it on a cool setting.
- You could follow the same process, using kitchen peelings – e.g. onion skins (brown and red onions give different colours), or avocado skins cut into shapes to print with.

PART 2

EARLY WINTER

END OF OCTOBER TO MID-DECEMBER

Autumn's coat is shedding:
slowly at first, then
seemingly all at once.

Temperatures dwindle along with the daylight, and darkness surrounds us once again. There's a scent of woodsmoke on the breeze and the orchards are ripening, filled with fruit ready for comforting crumbles. In the woods, wild mushrooms peep through a carpet of fallen leaves and pinecones.

While the arrival of autumn often seems gentle, a gradual turning golden of the land, winter's onset can feel comparatively sudden. The first of the season's storms can leave branches prematurely bare, the appearance of frost enforcing a swift end to the growing season, dreich weather dampening the ground and our collective mood alike.

Winter's arrival can be jarring to say the least – and it's probably why, in recent years, it feels like the whole of November has become an extended countdown to Christmas, rather than a transition between autumn and winter. Christmas trees appear suddenly in windows, festive music fills the shops and adverts for 'the Big Day' begin bombarding us on all fronts. If these things bring you joy, there's no judgement here – we need to find light in the dark in any way we can – but I can't help but wonder if this premature celebration of the festive season acts as something of a displacement and can actually be counter-intuitive.

Instead of sitting with the arrival of winter, letting ourselves land kindly in this time and gradually acclimatising to the darkness, we resist it. This is not always a conscious choice, of course, but a product of the modern world, and a habit we have developed over years – by being pushed to prepare for the festive season we are distracting ourselves with the next thing. But to resist the season we are in robs us of present joy and sets happiness as a distant bar, to be achieved on one day in December, fooling ourselves into believing that spring will magically be here after that. I know in the past I've often struggled most in November, which really can seem an endless month, and coped by buying things in the Black Friday sales and indulging in a Christmas film or two, keen to be through the darkness and out the other side of winter. Neither activity helped for long, a temporary dopamine hit leaving me feeling more discombobulated than ever. Stepping back, I realise now how much I was being manipulated by marketing, and that the consuming and comparing it invited me to do ultimately left me feeling even more down.

HONOURING THE SEASONS

I now embrace some gentle anticipation of the festive season, but also have some tools to ensure I don't forget the here and now too – tools I will explore in this section. We can bring out the fairy lights early but make lanterns of autumn leaves rather than hang baubles; plan our festive diary but host a dinner party now to give thanks for the final harvests; come up with a list of presents to make for Christmas and gently start, instead of panicking later and over-spending in the shops; we can preserve autumn's bounty now to share all winter long.

Rather than dreading it, we can meet this time with open minds and hearts to settle softly into the winter, rather than fighting against it. This transition between autumn and winter can be cocooning, if we let it; a gradual winding down that embraces the slowness of winter.

Our Celtic ancestors and the rituals and traditions they built around this time are very much in this spirit of acceptance. They truly honoured the seasonal shift and its fluid boundaries – between autumn and winter, life and death, the human and the divine. Samhain begins on the evening of 31 October and is the halfway point between the autumn equinox (Mabon) and the winter solstice (Yule). It was the third and final harvest festival and marked the beginning of winter with bonfires, feasting, dressing up and other rituals to appease the spirit world. While there are few written records about this time, we do know that Samhain dates back centuries – first being recorded in the Coligny calendar in the first century BC. As the evidence of these celebrations was often communicated by word of mouth rather than documented, many of the stories and legends passed down through the generations have been lost, making it even more important to cherish and share the ones remaining.

With these rich traditions of connection and existential significance, it's no wonder that this seasonal shift can bring with it a changing energy: it's one that can be productive and creative, if we give ourselves grace, but can sometimes feel overwhelming too. At this time of year, there can be a growing expectation to participate and be sociable – especially as Christmas approaches – but at the same time we might rather retreat home in the growing darkness. I know I've felt both the desire to be doing things and embrace the season but also to hibernate, sometimes simultaneously, and it can be disorientating and leave us feeling anxious and alone.

Outer Darkness, Inner Darkness

As Samhain approached in the winter after our elopement, I felt increasingly isolated. My first book had been published – it had been a long road to get there, and my world was fizzing with possibility. I found my quiet, introverted self suddenly thrust into the spotlight doing live radio interviews and writing vulnerable pieces about my mental health in Sunday supplements. I was being honest and raw in ways I have never been before, never mind so publicly. I wanted my words to reach the people who needed them, to try and make them feel less alone. I tried to hold onto this thought but was saying things out loud I had never said outside the therapy room. I had 'come out' with OCD for the first time to both strangers and friends, and was plagued by self-doubt and imposter syndrome. What's more, in the whirlwind of publishing alongside my busy teaching job, I was then very much not living the *Slow Seasons* mindset I so cherished. I was struggling to utilise the very coping mechanisms that I embraced in my writing, leaving me feeling lower than ever, not to mention guilty – as though I was some sort of fraud for not being able to embody the values I had written about.

I soon worked out there was another reason I was feeling so out of sorts. Something in my body felt different again. The week of publication, I took a pregnancy test – and suddenly there it was: two dark pink lines. We were going to have a baby.

Words can barely articulate how happy I was – it was everything I had always wanted, had longed for, for so long. But at the same time, it was like a switch had flicked: the anxiety and OCD that had faded to background characters in my mind suddenly crashed back onto centre stage. The thrum of the anxious interior monologue I had worked so hard to quieten became even louder than before, and I was plagued by constant intrusive thoughts about accidentally causing harm to the baby.

On the outside, everything looked perfect: my book was a bestseller before publication, and I was pregnant with our long-awaited baby. But inside, everything was in turmoil – I was all too aware of what was at stake. Life was so full-on: my stress levels were high, and I was expending huge effort masking my distress as I promoted my book online and in interviews. I was so busy I sometimes even forgot I was pregnant, then felt incredibly guilty, knowing that the stress wasn't good for the baby, feeling that if something bad happened it would all be my fault. Sleepless nights bled into restless days and my schedule continued at a frantic pace.

And then, as Samhain arrived, 'morning' sickness hit as we reached the climax of book promotion and I was plagued with nausea all day long. On the long journey back from a book event in St Andrews, I only just managed to hold in the vomit until we reached our front door. I felt trapped, unable to share the reason I was wracked with anxiety. I was counting down to the twelve-week scan, desperate to see that our baby was okay. My world grew darker and darker as daylight dwindled, and I had never felt more alone.

Creative Community Lights the Way

I had always found winter comforting – a time to take our cues from nature, embracing a slower pace and spend cosy time at home – but as I embarked on pregnancy it felt like I was staring down the barrel of a gun. I was overwhelmed with gratitude at managing to conceive but wrestled with guilt at not being able to enjoy this long-awaited season of my life. Outer darkness echoed inner darkness. In the past, I had struggled with winter before learning to embrace it, and in my matrescence the metaphor was all too apt – particularly as we descended into the dark heart of the year, daylight ever diminishing, yet the shortest day seemed so very far away.

Instead of fighting the darkness, I realised that I needed to slow down and feel my feelings, and in order to do so I had to succumb to the season I was in – taking it easier and embracing rest along with the outside world. I had to ask for help. I told my wonderful then-editor Kitty, who helped me manage the demands on my time, and a lovely new GP finally listened to my cries for help and made a referral to specialists in the perinatal mental health team. I put one foot in front of the other.

During this dark time, it was the very smallest things that brought me tiny glimmers of joy. A crisp walk on frosty mornings before the world was awake. The perfect ruby red of an acer leaf. A hot drink hugged between mittens. Turning on the fairy lights when I got home. Noticing their sound first, then looking up to observe the graceful 'V' shape of migrating geese in the sky. Noticing the beauty of a winter sunrise and sunset and the unique golden quality of that light in the gloaming just before dawn and dusk: a reminder that the sun would still rise, the world would still turn. That there was beauty in the darkness – even a beauty created by the darkness.

Another glimmer was community. Gathering in the way of my ancestors to host events, making things together with other like-minded old souls, and sharing stories, were all ways I came back to myself by meeting readers. They brought their vulnerability, and I shared my own. We admired the unexpected brightness of a rosehip or the perfect curl of a piece of bracken together, ate cake I had made with the season's first apples, swapped stories about our mental health and sheltered from storms together – quite literally – more than once.

I realised that these gatherings, often in circles with other women, offered us all a permission slip to step away from the daily grind, surround ourselves in nature and immerse ourselves in the act of creating. I could give myself leave to step away: from the stresses of my full-time teaching schedule, from my frantic Google searches about pregnancy symptoms, and from ruminating over our upcoming appointments and scans.

I started to take my own advice again, turning to the simplest of things in an attempt to still my racing mind. The likes of foraging for sea-buckthorn berries at the beach and the meditative stirring of a preserving pan offered promises to my future self – flashes of optimism in a time when it was in such short supply. Balancing these moments outdoors in nature and embracing cold noses and wet feet with time spent battening down the hatches and cosying up indoors were lifelines for me during a time that I felt completely out of control of my own body and mind.

That winter taught me that I had more strength than I thought. And I do believe that winter tries to teach us things, if we can take the time to listen carefully enough. Winter is imbued with its own quiet magic and rich with creative possibility if we allow ourselves permission to slow down and look for it. Samhain is a time to celebrate the final leaves falling: a beautiful reminder of our own place in nature, in the universe and the circularity of all things.

'WINTER IS IMBUED WITH ITS OWN QUIET MAGIC AND RICH WITH CREATIVE POSSIBILITY.'

STORIES FROM FOLKLORE

The beginning of winter is steeped in significance, associated with ritual traditions and spine-chilling folklore as the boundaries between our world and the Celtic Otherworld were believed to be thinnest, with spirits and fairies abundant. Samhain heralds the beginning of the darker half of the year as the final Gaelic harvest festival, celebrated on 31 October and 1 November. Some believe the holiday was Christianised in the eighth century and instead All Saint's Day or All Hallows' Day was celebrated on 1 November – the name All Hallows' Eve evolving into the Scots word 'Hallowe'en'. Traditions were taken across the pond to America, where they were mixed with other influences, including Mexico's Day of the Dead and the Roman festival of Pomona to become the Hallowe'en most of us now know.

Today's tradition of building bonfires around Hallowe'en relates to the folk tradition of lighting bonfires (known as 'samhnagan'; pronounced 'saow-anagan') to protect from evil spirits visiting that night and to hold them back until sunrise. Communities would have competitions to see who could build the largest bonfire, and they were often built on hills so that they could be seen across the land.

As apples are often associated with the dead and the Otherworld in Celtic and other mythologies, Samhain was sometimes referred to as the 'Feast of Apples'. One seasonal apple superstition involves burying apples or their pips by moonlight at Hallowe'en to feed the souls of the dead roaming the earth on the night of Samhain. 'Dookin'', 'ducking' or 'bobbing' for apples – extracting an apple from a large vessel of water without using your hands – is still a favourite Hallowe'en party game today and is thought to be an ancient tradition. Some people think it comes from the

Celtic belief that the Otherworld would be filled with the fruit and flowers of apple trees and was popularised by the Romans during the Pomona festival. Other stories say the game is related to the witch hunts, where witches were 'dooked' in water to find out if they were innocent. For more on apple folklore, see page 78.

These days, while the pointed hats and black cloaks of witches' costumes are ubiquitous during Hallowe'en, in the past being associated with witchcraft in Scotland would have been taboo at best, dangerous at worst. During the sixteenth and seventeenth centuries, witchcraft was a crime that thousands of people were accused of, and many were executed in the infamous witch trials. The majority of the accused were ordinary women, often servants to rich families, or farmers' wives. Strange happenings such as spoilt food or 'cursed' (diseased) livestock could result in accusations. Other allegations were brought against women thought to have evil powers from making a deal with the devil or partaking in demon worship. They were regarded as religious heretics and the accused were often tortured barbarically into 'confessing' their crimes, burned at the stake or 'dooked' in water – if they floated (as most people would), they were considered guilty.

Another Scottish Samhain tradition was for couples to burn hazelnuts on the bonfire. In folklore, the hazel is thought to represent wisdom and understanding, so if the nuts burned quietly and equally, the partnership would be content – but if they hissed or spat, the relationship was thought to be doomed. Turnips (or 'tumshies' in Scots) the size of a human head would be hollowed, carved with spooky faces and lit with candles to scare away evil spirits (see page 70).

In the eighteenth century – in the time of the Scottish Bard Rabbie Burns, who wrote about Samhain traditions in his poem 'Hallowe'en' – kale was also thought to be prophetic. Young folks would pull the hardy green vegetable from the ground after dark with blindfolds on and the length or shape of the stalk was believed to symbolise the build of your future lover. The state of the roots would indicate their future wealth or lack thereof – clean roots meant lean days, while clumps of soil suggested plenty. Another divination ritual involved toasted oats served with whipped cream in a concoction called 'fuarag na samhna', which had tokens folded into the mixture to predict the future. Guests would take turns to eat a spoonful of the pudding and find out their fate: a ring meant engagement, while a thimble meant singledom; a coin represented money, and a button lack thereof.

'Guising' is a Scottish Hallowe'en tradition whereby children would wear costumes (their disguises) such as sheepskins and masks and wigs of hay and pretend to be evil spirits visiting houses. Folks believed that at this time spirits and fairies could steal children, so the disguises were also thought to keep them safe. They would be given gifts to help protect them from evil in exchange for performing a song or other talent, such as a trick or a joke – hence the modern name 'trick-or-treating'.

'COMMUNITIES
WOULD HAVE
COMPETITIONS TO
SEE WHO COULD BUILD
THE LARGEST BONFIRE,
AND THEY WERE
OFTEN BUILT ON
HILLS SO THAT THEY
COULD BE SEEN
CROSS THE LAND.'

FINDING LIGHT

Pumpkin Folklore

These days, it's hard to think of this time of year without summoning images of pumpkins glowing in the dark, their flickering candles casting ghostly shadows on the wall. The stories of Samhain and the pumpkin intersect in the nineteenth century when the Jack-O'-Lantern took on its modern, recognisable form. Prior to this, lanterns with scary faces were carved from turnips or potatoes to scare away spirits, but when Irish immigrants arrived in America pumpkins were plentiful, not to mention easier to carve.

There are different stories about the origin of the lantern. The name 'Jack-O'-Lantern' was once used interchangeably with 'will-o'-the-wisp', the name for strange lights that appeared over bogs leading travellers into danger. The most popular story is the Irish folk tale of Stingy Jack, which tells of an unpleasant cheat who played tricks on people, including conning the devil out of money. His sin meant he found no place in heaven or in hell and condemned him to walk the Earth forever. In Scotland, turnips thrived in the cold, wet climate and were hollowed out, carved into frightening expressions and lit from the inside; they were called tumshie lanterns, and were thought to scare off evil spirits like Jack, particularly when the boundary between worlds was thinnest.

Pumpkins originated in Mexico around 9,000 years ago and were a staple food of Indigenous Americans, who grew them alongside beans and sweetcorn using the productive 'Three Sisters' method. There are over forty varieties of pumpkin in shades of forest green, bright red, vivid yellow and – of course – ubiquitous orange. Every part of the fruit is edible, and different varieties have different textures and flavours, lending themselves to different uses.

Pumpkin Guide

While all types of pumpkins are edible, some are tastier than others! A far reach from your standard supermarket carving pumpkin, bred for its size and perfect roundness but weak and watery in flavour, if you seek out culinary pumpkins from your local farmers' market or greengrocer, you will be richly rewarded. Not only do they have a variety of versatile uses, but they are much more interesting to look at as well, and make for a beautiful, natural autumn display without any adornment. Their season peaks in October and November, but they can last well into winter if stored carefully in a cool, dry spot.

Crown Prince
This striking pumpkin is a culinary favourite: it has silvery blue skin that conceals vivid orange flesh beneath. Its flavour is sweet and nutty, and it has a creamy texture when cooked. It's a versatile pumpkin to use in recipes, especially as it stores very well over winter – and can look really pretty on display to celebrate Samhain before you eat it too.

Kabocha

Also known as the Japanese pumpkin, this winter squash has a textured forest green or dark orange exterior, with light orange flesh. Its soft texture and sweet taste lend themselves superbly to Asian flavours and it is found a lot in these cuisines, for instance in tempura and *korokke* (croquettes). Its size and shape mean it is also a great candidate for slow roasting whole. It stores well, its flavour maturing and sweetening over time. Look out for Delica pumpkins grown in Italy – a premium variety of kabocha beloved by foodies for its concentrated flavour.

Acorn

This winter relative of summer squashes such as the courgette has a similar, milder flavoured yellow-orange flesh that works well in both sweet and savoury dishes; it is best roasted – either whole or cut into rings – to bring out its subtly nutty notes. Appropriately, it has a distinctive acorn shape with vertical ridges and is either dark green with a single orange splodge or variegated with orange, yellow and green stripes.

Onion Squash
This squash has a less savoury flavour than other pumpkins – it is almost chestnut-like in its subtle sweetness, hence its other name, *uchiki kuri* or red kuri squash, as *kuri* can refer to chestnuts in Japanese. It is small, reddish-orange in colour and has a pointed top like an onion. It is sometimes striped, and has thin skin, making it good for roasting in chunks or whole for stuffing to make the most of its velvety, dark orange flesh.

Turban Squash
This variety is an heirloom plant commonly grown in the past, but it can be a little harder to come by than other pumpkins nowadays. It has a unique appearance, with a vibrant, orange-red lower half and a hat-like top, often striped with green. It looks impressive but has a milder flavour than other varieties, so use as you would butternut squash – roasting brings out the best flavour.

Jill Be Little

This is a tiny pumpkin and a climbing variety, so great for growing in smaller spaces or in pots. You might find them in some florists for decorative purposes (alongside the ghostly white miniature Casperita) just make sure they haven't had anything added to them – plus, those bred for their looks can be a little tasteless. To get the most out of them, miniature pumpkins are best roasted whole with a sprinkling of evergreen herbs and sea salt.

Rouge Vif d'Etampes

A French heritage variety also known as the 'Cinderella Pumpkin' for its large size, orange-red skin and blocky shape, traditionally used on the Continent as a soup tureen. If you're looking for other, fairytale-esque varieties, Porcelain Doll is a peachy pink with exaggerated ribs and almost square shape, while Musquée de Provence is another French heirloom variety with deep ridges and orangey brown skin. These pumpkins taste sweet too – ideal for baking or making into soups or pies with warming spice.

'BEFORE PUMPKINS, TURNIP LANTERNS OR "TUMSHIES" WERE LIT TO SCARE OFF EVIL SPIRITS.'

SPICED PUMPKIN LOAF CAKE

Brown butter gives a rich, nutty flavour to baking. It is made by heating the butter to drive off the water content and caramelise the milk solids. The toffee notes of the brown butter pair perfectly with sweet pumpkin, which also gives the cake a lovely soft crumb, and cinnamon, which brings seasonal warmth. The cake is topped with a brown butter buttercream icing (try saying that quickly three times!) that brings just the right amount of sweetness.

Serves 12

For the cake:
Small butternut squash or pumpkin (or use tinned purée, see Tip)
120g unsalted butter
200g light soft brown sugar
2 tsp ground cinnamon
300g self-raising flour
2 large free-range eggs

For the buttercream:
120g unsalted butter
200g icing sugar
1 tbsp whole milk
1 tsp vanilla extract

First, make your pumpkin purée by peeling and chopping the butternut squash or pumpkin into 1cm chunks. Cook it in the microwave for 5–10 minutes with a little water, then drain it before blitzing with a hand blender until smooth. Weigh out 250g (see Tip for using any leftovers).

Next, brown your butter for both the cake and buttercream. Heat 240g of butter in a saucepan over a medium heat until melted. Keep heating the mixture, stirring all the while – the butter will start to foam. Keep going and you will see the milk solids changing colour at the bottom of the pan, floating as brown flecks to the surface and the liquid butter will turn golden and smell deliciously nutty. Take the pan straight off the heat.

Decant 100g of the brown butter into a large mixing bowl and add the remaining 100g into a separate bowl. Set both aside to cool.

Preheat the oven to 180°C/Fan 160°C/Gas Mark 4 and grease and line a 450g loaf tin.

To make the cake, add the pumpkin purée to the large mixing bowl of cooled brown butter and stir until well combined.

Stir in the brown sugar, followed by the cinnamon, self-raising flour and eggs, stirring between each addition.

Pour the mixture into the prepared tin, then bake in the oven for 45–50 minutes, until a skewer inserted in the middle comes out clean. Set aside to cool in the tin for a few minutes, then remove to cool completely on a wire rack.

Meanwhile, make the buttercream. Pour the remaining 100g brown butter into the bowl of a stand mixer, then add the icing sugar and beat until they just come together.

Add the milk and vanilla extract, then beat again for at least 5 minutes, until light and airy.

Once the cake has cooled completely, top with the buttercream. Dollop it on the surface of the cake, then smooth it out evenly with a palette knife.

Serve in slices with a cup of tea.

Tip

— Any extra pumpkin purée can be stirred through pasta, baked into bread or diluted with stock into a soup.
— You can use tinned pumpkin purée, which is usually more watery than making your own, so the baking time might be longer – set a timer and check after 50 minutes.

Apple Traditions

The apple tree, as well as its fruit, has strong connections with Scottish folklore, not only as a symbol of abundance and fertility but also as a link between the human world and the Celtic Otherworld – which is especially apt around Samhain when the boundaries between mortal and divine were believed to be thinner.

The wild apple tree – often found at the edge of forests – was thought to be a gateway of sorts to the mysterious Otherworld, while the apple itself was known as a symbol of rebirth; according to some stories, wild apples (*Malus sylvestris*) would be buried in graves as food for the dead as they were key to entering the afterlife. In Celtic folklore, apples symbolise wisdom and are associated with divine truth, as well as representing commitment and love. Some believed that if the pips were tossed into the fire and exploded as the lover's name was recited, their feelings were true. Romantically, the apple is part of the rose family, and its health-giving properties (vitamins, minerals and fibre) probably contributed to its perception as a magical fruit that restored anything – from youth to life itself – and its use in a variety of healing practices.

The European native crab apple or wild apple is the ancient forerunner of the apple we know today – *Malus domestica* and all its many varieties. The tree can live for hundreds of years, is recognisable for its gnarled, 'crabbed' look and is a happy home for lichens and parasitic mistletoe. While very sour to eat (though wildlife and cattle aren't so picky), in Scottish tradition the fruit would be foraged during the autumn months and the tiny, tart, hard apples would be boiled to extract the juice and pulp before being strained through a 'jeelie bag' that was handed down through the generations, then boiled again with sugar to make a russet-coloured crab-apple jelly.

Apple Guide

Ribston Pippin
'Pippin' means grown from seed, and namesake is a sweet, pear-flavoured apple that dates back to the 1700s. It gets regular mention in Victorian literature, from Conan Doyle to Dickens. It is the parent of the popular Cox's Orange Pippin, a variety that is easier to come by today and is known for its mottled red skin, crisp, tangy flesh and notes of aniseed. Both are harvested in mid- to late-September through to October.

Blenheim Orange
Also known as Kempster's Pippin, the Blenheim Orange also dates back to the 1700s and is distinctive in its dual use – as a cooking apple from late September (when it is great for making fine purées) then as an eating apple over winter as its flavour and sweetness develops. It has a greenish-yellow or orange skin striped with red, and the flesh has a characteristic nutty flavour.

Egremont Russet
Russet apples have skin that is covered in 'russeting' – rough patches of green or yellow-brown. While its outer appearance may not be something to write home about, the skin of the Egremont Russet conceals a nutty, fragrant fruit that has made it popular since Victorian times. They're also known as 'rusticoats' or 'leathercoats' – a term that dates back to Shakespeare's time. It thrives in the cold, can be harvested from October and keeps well.

Bloody Ploughman
The Bloody Ploughman is a distinctive Scottish variety that ripens relatively early and has a sweet flavour and deep red skin and flesh. The story goes that it got its name from a ploughman who was caught stealing apples from Megginch Estate in Perthshire and was shot dead by the gamekeeper. His widow supposedly found the apples and threw them on the compost, where they sprouted into a tree with bloody red fruit.

Dabinett
As craft cider production has become more widespread, old cider-making varieties such as Dabinett have seen a resurgence, especially in Somerset. The yellow-green fruit is harvested late in the apple-growing season and has a deeply sharp, bittersweet flavour that lends itself well to cider-making.

Worcester Pearmain
This variety was once the most popular early harvesting apple, and this quality has seen it used extensively in apple breeding. It is known for its sweet, strawberry-like flavour and has a pretty, crimson-flushed skin. Its descendants, such as Discovery, are now easier to come by. It also has lovely white, fragrant blossom in the springtime.

CARDAMOM APPLE BUTTER

Apple butter is a preserve that's made from apple purée reduced down with sugar and spices until caramelised and jammy. It is a great way to use up a glut of windfall apples – just be sure to cut away any bruises or damaged parts. It's delicious on porridge or to top toast or crumpets, used in baking or eaten straight from the jar with a spoon! As apple butter has less sugar than traditional preserves, I recommend decanting it into smaller jars to store – it will keep for around a month in the fridge once opened, and around a year unopened if stored in a cool, dry place.

Makes 5 x 200g jars
800g cooking apples
400ml apple juice
300–400g caster sugar
1–2 tsp ground cardamom

Wash the apples and roughly chop them into chunks – no need to peel or core.

Place the apple chunks into a large pan along with the apple juice and heat over a medium–low heat until it comes to a simmer.

Turn down the heat and cook gently with the lid on for around 30 minutes until the apples have completely broken down into a rough purée (you can use a potato masher to help it along).

Pass the purée through a sieve into a large bowl and discard the pips and skin left in the sieve. Weigh the fruit purée and transfer to a clean pan.

For every 100g of purée, add 40g sugar and ¼ tsp ground cardamom. Stir together.

Warm the spiced apple mixture over a low heat until the sugar has completely dissolved, and you can't feel any grainy bits. Increase the heat to medium–high and allow the mixture to bubble away, stirring occasionally until it turns a slightly darker, more caramelised colour, reduces slightly and thickens – this will take around 15–20 minutes (note: if you are increasing the quantities and using a really big pot, this will take longer).

Meanwhile, preheat your oven to 110°C/100°C Fan/Gas Mark ¼ and sterilise your jars by washing them with warm soapy water and drying them in the oven. Boil the lids in a pan of water to sterilise them too.

Once your apple butter has thickened, take the pan off the heat, decant the mixture into the sterilised jars and seal immediately.

Late Autumn Foraging

Hazelnuts
Hazelnuts are known to have grown in the British Isles since the end of the Ice Age. In Celtic folklore, the hazel was thought of as a magical tree that could protect communities from evil. The tree is known as the 'Tree of Knowledge' in Ireland and associated with wisdom and inspiration in Scotland too. A rod of hazel was thought to be magical, used in divination rituals and to remedy various illnesses, including toothache. It's clear to see why these mythical-looking nuts were regarded as magical.

Hazel trees are native to the UK and have oval-shaped, double-tooth-edged leaves with a pointed end and hairy texture in the growing season. They turn yellow in the autumn, and as the leaves change colour, their clusters of oval hazelnuts – also known as cobnuts or filberts, depending on the variety – ripen. Hazelnuts grow in papery coverings called bracts in groups of between one and four and ripen as autumn deepens, ready to harvest in September and October when their papery covering begins to peel away from the nut. When fully mature they turn a deep brown. You can also pick them when they are young and green and ripen them at home somewhere warm and sheltered, meaning you're more likely to beat the squirrels or dormice to them. Before eating, their hard shell must be removed.

Sea-buckthorn
Sea-buckthorn is a spiky, evergreen shrub native to cold, coastal areas of Europe and Asia. It has bright, abundant orange berries in the autumn, known for their distinctive, sharp flavour and health-giving qualities thanks to the many vitamins and minerals they contain. Sea-buckthorn is found in sand dunes, often on the East coast of the UK, and is also known as sea berry and sandthorn (due to its habitat and appearance), or swallowthorn (after its avian neighbours who frequent the dunes). They are considered invasive, good at propping up sand dunes but form dense, spiky areas that can prevent other plants from thriving.

You wouldn't think such a small berry would pack such a flavour punch, but the berries themselves have an unexpectedly tropical note. This is foraging mindfulness at its most sensory: spotting the best patches of bright berries against the silvery grey leaves and ochre sand to focus a busy mind, enjoying the beautiful citrus scent as you gather them, and tasting a berry or two to wake up your taste buds.

HAZELNUT MILLIONAIRE'S SHORTBREAD

Scottish shortbread originated in the twelfth century, with its most modern and tasty iteration thanks to Mary, Queen of Scots in the sixteenth century. In the nineteenth century, people started adding ingredients such as nuts and candied fruit to shortbread. This recipe is adapted from one my mum made in her domestic science class back in the 1970s – a go-to sweet treat that is worth the extra effort of mindfully stirring the caramel on the stove. That said, this is a stir-together caramel, so doesn't demand thermometers or other fancy equipment, just a wee bit of extra attention. Here, I've tempered the sweetness of the chocolate with crunchy, earthy hazelnuts and just a pinch of salt.

Makes 16 squares

For the shortbread:
240g plain flour
80g caster sugar
160g cold butter, cut into cubes

For the caramel:
115g butter
115g light soft brown sugar
200ml condensed milk
2 tbsp golden syrup

For the topping:
50g blanched hazelnuts
200g milk chocolate
A couple pinches of sea salt flakes

First, make the shortbread. Preheat the oven to 180°C/Fan 160°C/Gas Mark 4. Grease and line a 20cm square baking tin with a depth of at least 5cm.

In a large bowl, mix together the flour and sugar, then rub in the butter with your fingertips until it resembles the texture of breadcrumbs.

Working lightly, knead the mixture together in the bowl until it forms a rough dough. Press the mixture into the bottom of the prepared tin with the tips of your fingers until it is an even thickness and reaches the edges of the tin – make sure to push it right into the corners. Prick the surface of the shortbread with a fork.

Roughly chop your hazelnuts into small pieces and place in a heatproof dish.

Bake the shortbread for 25–30 minutes on the middle shelf of the oven, until light golden brown (the dough might still feel a tad soft, but it will firm up as it cools). At the same time, roast the hazelnuts until golden brown, keeping an eye on them towards the end of the baking time to make sure they don't burn, and remove from the oven along with the shortbread. Set both aside to cool in their receptacles.

To make your caramel, combine all the caramel ingredients in a heavy-bottomed pan and melt together over a low heat until the sugar has dissolved. Raise the temperature to a medium heat, then bring the mixture to a boil, stirring constantly until it thickens a little and darkens to a caramel colour – about 5–10 minutes.

Pour the caramel over the top of the shortbread, spreading it evenly over the surface with a spatula if you need. Set aside to cool completely.

To make your topping, melt the chocolate in short bursts in the microwave or in a heatproof bowl over a pan of boiling water. Stir until melted and glossy. Mix in the chopped roasted hazelnuts, then pour over the top of the caramel. Sprinkle with a little sea salt then leave to set.

Cut into 16 squares and serve with a cup of tea.

SEA-BUCKTHORN CURD

You can buy sea-buckthorn juice, but it can be costly, thanks to the effort expended in collecting the berries. Instead, why not make gathering sea-buckthorn a mindful activity? When ripe, the berries are prone to bursting easily, so I recommend snipping off small branches to take home, then popping them in the freezer to make them easier to remove, or juicing them straight into the pan wearing heavy duty gloves! Just a little juice can make a delicious curd – for a silky topping for toast, layering sponge cakes or to fill pastry cases – that tastes like a cross between passionfruit and blood orange.

Makes approx. 180ml

3 tbsp sea-buckthorn juice (see Tip)
75g caster sugar
55g butter
1 large, free-range egg

First, sterilise a 180ml jar by washing it in hot, soapy water, rinsing it well and leaving it to dry in the oven at 110°C/Fan 100°C/Gas Mark ¼. Sterilise the lid by boiling it in a pan of water.

To make the curd, add the juice and sugar to a small pan and warm over a low heat until the sugar has dissolved.

Add the butter and heat until just melted. Whisk the egg and add to the curd, be sure to keep mixing it constantly as you do so, or you will scramble the egg in the heat.

Continue to whisk the curd over a low heat until it thickens and coats the back of a spoon, around 10 minutes. Decant into the sterilised jar and seal immediately.

Stored in the sterilised jar, it should keep for a couple of months. Once opened, store in the fridge – it will keep for a week or two.

Tip

– To make your own sea-buckthorn juice, wash the berries and cover them with a little water in a heavy-bottomed pan. Simmer until the berries burst, encouraging them to give up their juices by mashing them. Once the fruit has cooked and the berries have all burst, sieve the mixture to remove the seeds and use as desired.

AUTUMN LEAF LANTERN

There's something so satisfying about a craft made with materials you already have around the house, and these jam jars decorated with autumn leaves make for a simple but effective autumn lantern. The candlelight shines through the translucent leaves, highlighting their distinctive shapes and beautiful colours. For this craft I favour leaves with interesting silhouettes for the most impact, but experiment with different colours and shapes for different effects. I've used a LED candle for this craft as not all jars are designed to cope with the heat from a candle and could crack or even explode, especially if the tealight moves and accidentally touches the side. If you want to make this craft with candles you can light, make sure you use a jar made from heat-resistant glass such as one for preserving, and make sure the tea light is centred at all times.

You will need:
Recycled glass jar
Autumn leaves
Small paint brush
Decoupage glue (see Tip below)
LED tealight

Make sure your glass jar is scrupulously clean and dry, both inside and out.

For best results, clean your autumn leaves to make sure there is no dirt on their surface, then press them between sheets of kitchen roll under a stack of heavy books for several hours, or overnight.

Using your paintbrush, cover the outside of the glass jar with a thin layer of glue.

Consider the placement of your leaves; once you have decided where they will go, press them firmly, one at a time, onto the glue-covered outer surface of the jar.

Carefully coat each of the leaves with another layer of glue on top (it will dry clear but will seal the leaf to preserve it and stop it drying out).

Allow the glue to dry for several hours or overnight.

When you're ready to use your leaf lantern, place the LED tealight inside the jar and enjoy.

Tip

— If you don't have decoupage glue, you can use PVA glue thinned with a little water and a coat of varnish to protect the finished lantern.

EMBRACING DARKNESS

Fire Folklore

Fire has an important role in Celtic folklore. The hearth was the heart of the home, for gathering together in the warmth, to eat and to share stories. Fire was regarded as sacred, representing protection and purification as well as the cycle of life. Symbolic fires bookend the dark half of the year, associated with its Samhain beginnings, as winter started in earnest, and also the start of Celtic summer, in Beltane fire customs.

Ritual bonfires were used to communicate the arrival of Samhain and became the site of feasting and revelry, providing light, warmth and hope during a time of literal and metaphorical darkness. As well as to huddle around, share folk tales and legends and keep warm in the cold of early winter, they had a symbolic function: to welcome the spirits of ancestors and protect against the evil gods, fairies and witches people believed roamed the land during Samhain. A place was often left for the souls of dead relatives, with offerings of bread to show they were remembered. Livestock would be cleansed by walking between bonfires, and sometimes purifying herbs were burned in the flames. Divination rituals would also take place around the bonfire (see page 60) and torches were carried around communities to protect them from evil.

Outwith these specific festivals, so-called 'need-fires' (known as 'tein'-éigin' in Scottish Gaelic) would be lit during times of sickness (such as the plague or when there were outbreaks of disease in cattle) or danger, thought to be physically and spiritually cleansing. In Highland communities, these fires were built annually to ward off possible disaster and sick animals would sometimes be burned sacrificially. The need-fire would be lit with an oak 'fire drill', then built into a large bonfire, which in turn lit the hearth fires of the entire community via torches. The ashes were thought to bring protection and would be sprinkled over the fields or boiled up with water to douse sick members of the community and livestock. There were many superstitions around the fire, such as requiring other nearby fires to be extinguished, and nine men to build it for luck.

NATURAL FIRELIGHTERS

While fire once meant light and life in the depth of winter, if you don't depend on it for either of these things, making one can be a mindful activity to calm busy minds. There is joy to be found in sorting the logs, collecting the kindling, building a pyramid or box, coaxing flames from the wood and fanning the fire into life. If – like me – you need a helping hand to breathe life into your fire, then firelighters are a must. A natural alternative to shop-bought firelighters can be made from soy wax, soy wicks, and some botanical ingredients to kindle the flames – and has the bonus of bringing natural scent too. Dried pinecones are lovely for creating a cosy autumnal atmosphere, while dried orange slices, cinnamon sticks and star anise evoke the festive season to come.

You will need:
A cupcake tray
Cupcake cases
Soy wicks with adhesive metal buttons at the bottom
Soy wax pellets
Dried botanicals (clean and free of dirt): dried herbs or flowers, small dried (open) pinecones, dried orange slices or spices such as cinnamon sticks or star anise

Preheat the oven to 120°C/Fan 100°C/Gas Mark ½. Line the cupcake tray with cupcake cases (this makes the firelighters easier to remove).

Stick a wick in the middle of the bottom of each case, then fill the cupcake cases with wax pellets almost up to the top of each case. If the wick is very long you may need to trim it to around 3cm above the top of the case.

Place the tray on the middle shelf of the oven until the wax has melted – around 10 minutes.

Remove the cupcake tray from the oven and gently place your dried botanicals into the melted wax, placing them around the wick. The wax will rise up, so be careful not to let it overflow.

Leave the tray at room temperature to allow the wax to solidify, then remove the firelighters from the tray and peel away the cupcake cases.

To use, place your firelighter underneath your kindling and light the wick to ignite it.

Tip

– Store your firelighters near the hearth ready to light fires, but make sure they are in a sealed, heatproof jar so they don't melt or lose their scent.

HAND-DIPPED BEESWAX CANDLES

Burning beeswax candles is a truly sensory experience: their honey-rich scent, the warm glow they produce as they burn, the soft, malleable feel of the natural wax. Something about their golden light and comforting scent makes them well-suited to the darker half of the year. Beeswax has been used in lighting for thousands of years and burns with a naturally bright light the same spectrum as the sun – offering much-needed warm light in winter, as well as a comforting connection back to past ritual. Mindfully melting the wax and the rhythmic dipping and rolling of the candles is incredibly grounding.

I like to use household objects I already have to hand for crafts; I first learnt the tennis ball tube trick from my friend Nathalie a few years ago, and have used it ever since.

You will need:
A heavy-bottomed pan (one you don't mind getting messy)
A tall metal can, for example a metal tennis ball tube
Beeswax pellets
A roll of cotton wick
A craft knife
A heatproof mat or surface
Newspaper or scrap paper

Fill your pan with a few centimetres of water and place your tall tin filled three-quarters of the way up with beeswax into the water to form a makeshift double boiler.

Over a medium heat, bring the water to the boil. While the wax begins to melt, measure and cut your wick: you will dip two candles at a time, so work out how long you want your candle to be, double this and add 3cm.

When the wax has melted, transfer the can to your heatproof surface. Fold your wick in two, leaving 3cm in the middle to hold. Dip one end of the wick straight up and down in the tin can. For the first dip, you might need to wiggle the wick around a little until it's coated with wax. Leave any excess to drip into the can for a few seconds, then repeat with the other side, leaving 3cm between the dipped ends.

Allow to cool slightly, then roll the candles on your heatproof surface, smoothing them out using your fingers by moving them up and down the length of the candle in a rolling motion to ensure an even finish. Allow to cool a little more.

Now you have coated the wick, you can dip both candles at once, and with each dip it will get easier to cover the surface of the forming candles. Holding them by the uncovered middle section of wick, dip both candles straight down and back up in the wax in one confident movement to avoid bubbles and blemishes forming on the surface of the candle.

Repeat the process of rolling and smoothing. You might need to trim the end with a craft knife every few dips to avoid a bulge of wax forming at the bottom of your candle that has no wick and so will not burn.

Keep repeating until you reach your desired thickness. About 10–12 dips will result in a classic dinner candle. Trim the bottom of the candles one last time and hang the pair of candles over newspaper or scrap paper to set.

Leave to cure for a week or so for a better burn and scent.

HONEY HONEYCOMB

Honeycomb, cinder toffee, sea foam, hokey pokey... different places have different names for this explosive, crunchy, caramelised sweet treat made by combining very hot sugar with bicarbonate of soda. In Scotland, it's called 'puff candy' because of its airy texture. Making it does require a little extra attention (thanks to the boiling sugar!) but is easier than you might think and makes for a lovely treat to eat around the bonfire or as a homemade gift. Make sure you use a big pan as it bubbles up more than you might expect! Inspired by Edinburgh-based chocolatier Edward & Irwyn, I like adding honey to mine instead of the traditional golden syrup, which gives the sweetness added complexity.

Makes approx. 125g
35g honey
100g demerara sugar
1 tsp bicarbonate of soda

First, line a high-sided 15 x 10cm heatproof dish.

Measure the demerara sugar and honey into a heavy-bottomed pan.

Over a low heat, melt the honey and sugar together slowly until the sugar has dissolved.

Turn up the heat and allow the mixture to bubble for 5–10 minutes until it is a dark caramel colour.

Remove the pan from the heat, then, taking care as the mixture will bubble up a lot, mix in the bicarbonate of soda with a wooden spoon until the raising agent is well combined.

Carefully – but quickly – decant the honeycomb into the prepared dish. It will continue to bubble. Set aside to cool completely, then cut into rough pieces.

Tip

— Make sure you store your honeycomb in a sealed container in a cool, dry place or it will go sticky very quickly.

PEAR AND STEM GINGER CAKE

Slices of warmly spiced, treacle-rich ginger cake wrapped in brown paper will always make me think of this time of year, enjoyed by the bonfire with a flask of something warming. This recipe is adapted from one of my gran's that I still have, written in her hand, dog-eared and batter-splattered from decades of use. She called this gingerbread, but it is a cake – the kind of cake that sticks to your ribs and warms you from the inside. It's an easy melt-together and mix recipe, and the smell is pure autumn. I've included stem ginger for added spice and seasonal pear for a fruity twist on my gran's traditional recipe.

Serves 8–10

225g self-raising flour
110g light soft brown sugar
1 tsp ground ginger
80g golden syrup
80g treacle
1 tbsp stem ginger syrup
180ml whole milk
85g butter
1 large, free-range egg
2 pears (approx. 275g), peeled, cored and chopped into 1cm chunks
2 balls of preserved stem ginger in syrup, chopped into very small pieces.

Preheat the oven to 190°C/Fan 170°C/Gas Mark 5 and grease and line a 20cm round, deep tin. Mix the dry ingredients together with a wooden spoon in a large bowl.

Add the golden syrup, treacle, stem ginger syrup, milk and butter to a medium-sized pan and melt slowly over a low heat until well combined. Set aside to cool slightly.

Beat the egg in a jug and add to the wet ingredients.

Pour the wet ingredients into the dry ingredients and mix well – the batter will be very runny. Fold in the pear and stem ginger.

Pour the mixture into the prepared tin and bake for approx. 45–50 minutes, until a skewer inserted in the middle comes out clean. Set aside to cool for a few minutes, then remove from the tin to serve warm, or allow to cool fully on a wire rack.

Tip

— Custard is a must if you're serving this warm for dessert!

Mushroom Folklore

Mushrooms have a strong connection with folklore in the UK, especially in Scotland; perhaps because of their potentially deadly properties and magical appearance, they are most often associated with fairies and supernatural creatures. The fly agaric (see overleaf) is one most often linked with fairies, who were thought to use them as dining tables or chairs for their feasts, and even as umbrellas during rainy spells. A perfect circle of mushrooms is referred to as a fairy ring or pixie ring. In Scotland, some people once believed that mushroom rings were formed when fairies danced in a circle and were best avoided: if you joined in, they would punish you in an eternal dance or even transport you to the fairy realm where you could become trapped. The phenomenon is, however, a natural one – thought to be a single mushroom that produces its fruiting bodies in a ring. They are most often found in woodlands, but you might also see them in grassy areas after inclement weather.

Fungi were also associated with witches – especially the likes of the bird's nest fungus or scarlet elf cups – and thought to bring a curse, being blamed for failed harvests and similar. The disgusting-looking, aptly named stinkhorn mushroom (or Witch's Egg) was also thought to bring bad luck, and if a yellow brain fungi (Witch's Butter) appeared at your threshold, people thought they had been put under a spell that would only be broken when the fungi disappeared.

While some mushrooms grow all year round, they are most abundant in the late autumn, with October being a peak time for many varieties to appear, a harbinger of winter to come. Damp weather and cooler temperatures provide ideal conditions for them to fruit, especially on the forest floor. Fungi are such a vital but often overlooked part of the woodland ecosystem, thriving on decaying leaf matter and transforming waste into nutrients that they pass onto nearby trees and other species via their roots through a magical – and still under-researched – system called the mycelium. Mushrooms or toadstools are the fruiting bodies of fungi, which produce spores to allow them to reproduce in certain conditions.

I don't think I'd feel confident foraging anything other than chanterelles – distinctive with their golden colour, fruity, apricot scent, wavy, funnel-like caps, false gills and pure white flesh inside (though still not to be confused with false chanterelles which have true gills, smell milder and have yellow or orange flesh). Even then, I'd probably err on the safe side and get them at the farmers' market instead. If you do want to forage mushrooms to eat then please do so with an expert as some species can be confused with potentially deadly consequences.

Rather than using this list as a guide to identify culinary mushrooms, here are some that I love to spot and enjoy their magic without picking them – usually by sketching or photographing them, or simply spending time in the special places that they grow. Mushrooms are a reminder of nature's cycle and our ability to find growth and life in the darkest, most unlikely of places. When there is very little thriving in nature, fungi are a reminder to look closely – in this case, beneath your feet – to find evidence of nature's fortitude.

Fly Agaric
Amanita muscaria
Think of a mushroom and its likely you will conjure up an image in your mind of the spotted fly agaric mushroom with its fairytale-esque appearance. It is a vivid, unmissable red, with white spots on its cap and is mainly found in woodland areas across the UK: look closely beneath birch, pine or spruce trees to find them. They are poisonous and were previously used as an insecticide.

Scarlet Elf Cup
Sarcoscypha austriaca
The bright pop of red from the scarlet elf cup is unmissable, especially as branches grow bare. They are very literally named, with a bright red or orange, cup-shaped cap. They grow on short stems that attach to decayed wood, especially after rain, and decaying branches and twigs on the forest floor or on the banks of streams. They are not poisonous, but they are regarded as inedible.

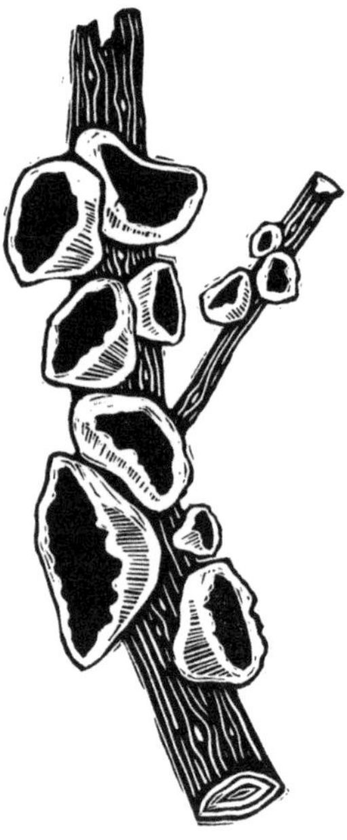

Jelly Ear

Auricularia auricula-judae

Another mushroom that appears as if straight out of a fairytale, jelly ear mushrooms look like little earlobes growing on damp, decaying branches in the shade. They have a distinctive squashy flesh that is almost velvety on the outside in an earthy reddish-brown colour and can be found on elder, ash, beech and sycamore trees. Jelly ears can be confused with poisonous species.

Oyster Mushroom

Pleurotus ostreatus

Large oyster mushrooms are obviously named for their fan-like cap. They are common throughout UK woodlands, especially on deciduous trees such as beech. They are cultivated, and can be found in shops for consumption, with a delicious scent of aniseed. Oyster mushrooms are actually carnivorous and consume small worms.

Common Puffball
Lycoperdon perlatum
The common puffball has tiny bumps that cover its outer surface and is white at first, maturing to yellow or brown. It grows in woodland leaf litter and grassy areas. On maturity, the puffball releases its spores through a hole in the top when touched by falling rain or passing animals. They are inedible as they mature and can be confused with poisonous species.

Common Bird's Nest
Crucibulum laeve
The bird's nest fungus has a tiny cup-like cap with what looks like a collection of small white eggs in the bottom. They are only 4–10mm across and appear in groups. They love decaying wood of all kinds, including bark chips, and can be found in parks and gardens – if you're looking closely enough!

Common Inkcap
Coprinopsis atramentaria
When the common inkcap decays, it creates a dark, oily liquid that was once used as a source of valuable ink. Its cone-like brownish-grey caps have tufted edges that appear to drip and it grows in groups, usually appearing after rain on decomposing wood or on damp grass in gardens and green spaces. It is poisonous in combination with alcohol, hence the folk name 'tippler's bane'.

FELT MUSHROOM DECORATION

Crafting with felt sheets is so nostalgic to me and is a great way to immortalise your mushroom spotting in craft form. Even better, felt doesn't fray so there's no faffing with hems or finishing, just a simple and decorative whip stitch to hold the shapes together. It was the Victorians who introduced fly agaric motifs to Christmas cards, as they felt it brought luck, and some people even believe it inspired Santa Claus' palette. While these felt mushroom decorations are lovely displayed around your house during the autumn, they will also look at home hung on your Christmas tree later, especially if you embellish them with a few beads to catch the light.

You will need:
Pencil
Paper
Scissors
Pins
Felt sheets (red and white, or colours of your choice)
Embroidery needle
Embroidery thread in a contrasting colour (e.g. white)
Ribbon (10cm long)
Wadding, fabric scraps or cotton wool balls
Fabric glue

Draw a simple outline of a mushroom on a piece of paper and cut around it.

Pin your mushroom pattern onto the felt, close to the edge and cut around the shape. Repeat to cut out a second mushroom shape.

Thread your needle with enough thread to go all the way round your shape (for a 6cm decoration you will need approx. 120cm): feed one end of the embroidery thread halfway through until the ends meet, then tie the ends in a knot.

Make a loop with the ribbon and place between the mushroom felt shapes, one on top of the other, making sure the edges match on both sides. The fabric on top as you sew will be the back, as the stitches will be more visible. Pin the shapes into place.

Next to the ribbon, about 2mm from the edge of the felt, poke your needle through the top layer of fabric only from the underside to the top, and pull the thread through until the knot is concealed between the layers of felt.

Now you're going to make your first stitch to sew the layers together, forming a loop around the edge of the felt: place your needle underneath the bottom layer of fabric and poke your needle through just underneath the knot and pull to tighten (though not so much that it puckers the felt).

Make your second stitch by poking your needle up through both layers of felt from underneath, this time at a 45-degree angle to the fabric and catching the ribbon so that it comes out about 5mm along from the first stitch and attaches your ribbon. Pull the thread tight again. This makes a stitch that is straight up and down the edge of the felt.

Repeat the process again, poking the needle through both layers of felt from underneath, starting underneath the place where the thread is coming out of the top and angling the needle so that it comes out 5mm away from the last stitch again and the wraps are perpendicular to the edge.

Repeat almost all the way round the shape, leaving a small gap to fill the shape with the padding or cotton wool, making sure it is well distributed and not lumpy.

Finish sewing the edge, and make the final stitch by poking your needle through both layers straight up (instead of at an angle) and finish off the thread by poking your needle through the bottom layer only, then tie a knot and use the needle to poke it in between the layers, before trimming the thread to release your needle.

To decorate with spots, cut out circles of felt in your contrast colour in various sizes and place them on the top of your mushroom, as desired, then glue in place with fabric glue.

Tip

— If you want, you could make the cap of your mushroom red and the stem white, by cutting out different colours and sewing the top to the bottom with a running stitch before sewing the two halves of the mushroom together so that the running stitch is concealed between the layers.

HOWE O

THE YEAR

The darkest days of winter,
the Howe o'the Year,
Midwinter, has arrived.
An ending and a beginning.
One year closes, and
another is born.

Here in Edinburgh, on the shortest day of the year on 21 or 22 December, sunrise takes place at around 8.40 a.m. and sunset at 3.40 p.m. That's only seven hours of daylight each day. Many of us start and finish work in the dark, so it can feel like there's little light to be found. Relentless dark days can leave us feeling drained and exhausted. Paired with dreary weather, storms and freezing cold temperatures, it's little surprise that our mood can be low.

It's understandable then that so many of us look forward to the festive season and all its sparkle as the high point of winter celebration. However, recent research has found that Christmas itself can leave many of us out in the cold, feeling money worries, present-buying stress, family difficulties and loneliness. It's no wonder that changes in routine and the way in which Christmas can fail to live up to the images depicted in adverts and on social media can lead to festive overwhelm and exacerbate seasonal depression.

And yet, if we pause to take stock and look around outside, the bare trees, quiet skies and short days offer up glimmers: a reminder to tap into the slowness of the season too. We are part of nature after all, and reframing this time as one of stillness and quiet, a lull in the day-to-day and a moment to reflect on what's important – whatever that means to you in this season – can be a way to counteract the overwhelm. An invitation from the great outdoors to hunker down and stay a while, to mark the darkest day and find solace in the knowledge that the light is growing once more.

December Darkness

When living through times of personal darkness, I know all too well that finding glimmers of light in the darkening days can be hard, the world outside seeming to add an extra layer of melancholy. As November gloom gave way to the pitch black of December in the winter of my pregnancy, my nausea and sickness continued to debilitate me, along with the daily effort to mask my distress. I navigated the world on high alert, envisioning dangers at every turn; I imagined the many harms I had done to the baby; I monitored every fragment that entered my mouth; I sought constant reassurance from my husband. My light dimmed further.

My community midwife, Carol, was my guardian angel and pushed for the help she could see I so badly needed. When I was eventually seen briefly by the local mental health service, I was left in an even worse state after one therapist asked me how long pregnancy lasted (yes, really – they didn't know) and questioned my ability to engage with the service in my 'condition'.

Advent arrived, along with our twelve-week scan. On a bitterly cold winter morning we pulled into the maternity carpark at the Royal Infirmary. My stomach swirled with a heady mix of terror and the two litres of water I'd been asked to down before the scan. I was promptly sick next to the car.

In spite of my overwhelming panic, I will never forget the moment we saw the baby. They were actually real – I hadn't harmed them. Miraculously, mercifully, and in spite of my darkest thoughts, all was well. A tiny, growing bundle of hope and energy. I breathed a little lighter.

Telling close family brought its own joy but my anxiety soon ramped up once more as everything suddenly seemed more real. The lead up to Christmas that year felt distinctly unjoyful, the world of shadows outside mirroring my internal darkness. When the day arrived, I struggled to eat a micro portion of Christmas dinner, roast potatoes stuck in my throat between waves of nausea.

On Hogmanay (the last day of the old year, 31 December, and the Scots name for New Year celebrations) we stayed in, a quiet night, but by 6 a.m. on New Year's Day my husband was awake with a winter vomiting bug. I was still being sick and cleaning up after both of us with a handkerchief over my mouth. I felt bleak. Was this a sign of the year to come?

New Beginnings, Old Ways

When I was struggling with my mental health during the depths of winter, I turned to the traditions of the solstice to light the way, traditions which predate Christmas by many thousands of years. The symbolism of the Howe o'the Year – the darkest day and longest night – spoke to me. Our ancestors celebrated the turning of the year in late December as a marker in the sand, a time to herald positive changes to come. Their traditions can offer glimmers of light at the darkest time in the seasonal cycle, even today.

In Highland folklore, the solstice is referred to in Gaelic as 'Grian-stad Geamhraidh', which means 'sun-stop winter'. The Celts viewed this time as a pause and a beginning: the moment after which the days start to get a little less dark, a turning point signalling the return of light and warmth. This was particularly pivotal in the past when our ancestors relied heavily on the land: the weather and the seasons had a profound impact on day to day lives, on the food on the table and on the ability to trade or barter – in other words, winter was, quite literally, about life and death. Reaching the shortest day of the year, and surviving, meant the darkest nights had passed. It meant celebrating the return of the light, little by little, one day at a time. To me, there's something beautifully comforting about this knowledge, this incremental progress, this certainty.

What's more, the Howe o'the Year has taken precedence in the Scottish calendar as Christmas was banned here for just over 300 years. In 1640, Protestant reformer John Knox made celebrating the Christian holiday punishable by imprisonment, as it was regarded as extravagant and sinful. Christmas festivities were deeply discouraged for centuries, and 25 December only became a public holiday in Scotland in 1958, meaning going to work on Christmas Day is still part of living memory.

As such, the celebration of Midwinter (also referred to as Yule) and Hogmanay took priority, lasting for many days. Once again, fire and feasting were a key part of celebrations, as with many of the traditions in the Celtic calendar. This was particularly important in Midwinter, since animals who wouldn't survive the harshest months of the year were slaughtered and meat would be plentiful. In the north of Scotland especially, where daylight at such latitudes can last only six hours, if that, fire festivals were common as the return of the light was so keenly celebrated. The best-known Scottish fire festival is Shetland's Up-Helly-Aa – which is now celebrated on the last Tuesday in January but historically stemmed from Yule and New Year celebrations – during which a Viking longship is set on fire, and feasting and revelry take over the capital, Lerwick. There are torchlit processions and fire-themed events across Scotland to see in the New Year, from Stonehaven Fireball Ceremony in the north to the Biggar Bonfire in the south. Clearly the symbolism of fire in all its light, warmth and protective capacity has had the power to bring Scottish communities together in the darkness for thousands of years.

Glimmers in Folklore and Nature

There are many magical ancient sites in Scotland with monuments or cairns that align with the light of the setting sun on the shortest day, believed to be places of ceremonial gathering and ritual to celebrate the changing of the seasons. The most famous of these is 5,000-year-old Maeshowe in Orkney, a chambered tomb and one of the finest Neolithic buildings to survive in northwest Europe. From the outside, it looks like an unassuming mound of grass ('howe' meaning hill), but inside is a large stone chamber, with just a small glint of light that enters the central part of the cairn as the setting sun aligns with the chamber during Midwinter. The careful positioning of its sloping passages, which were built to aim the light towards the back of this central chamber for the three weeks before and three weeks after the solstice, shows that Midwinter was a special time for the community (and extended well into the new year). Huge effort was expended to make the monumental tomb by moving and manipulating such massive stones, demonstrating the social commitment and powerful symbolism of the sun in Midwinter. There are different theories about the light and its meaning – some think it transported the souls of the dead, while others believe it was simply a calendar to remind islanders that the darkest time of year had passed, and the light was returning. Today, it still has a magical allure: viewers from around the world tune into the live stream to watch this significant moment on the winter solstice.

There are many high points of the Midwinter season in the Scottish calendar, but the surviving traditions that speak to me most are simpler, quieter ones such as the baking of the spiced Yule bread. Making and baking and the ingredients of the season have been key to Midwinter traditions for centuries and are a vital part of the darkest months for me. Even as a child, food was one of the best things about this time of year, and not just eating Granda's chocolate decorations from the Christmas tree before breakfast. I feel as though nature knows we need bounty in our kitchens at this time, and so many special ingredients have a micro-season or are at their best in and around December: whether rich chestnuts to roast on the fire or evergreen herbs to stir into sauces. From overseas, the leafy clementines, tangy cranberries and jewel-like pomegranates bring colour and flavour to the kitchen during Midwinter.

Time outside around the solstice is vital to me, and this is when I go foraging for my festive foliage, bringing in the symbolic evergreens to add natural, simple decor to my home, paired with beeswax candles and thrifty decorations such as paper bag stars. Winter roses bloom in time for Yule, and birds such as tawny owls and robins are easier to spot through bare branches. There are still some berries hanging on for the birds too, and their symbolism is also important – for instance, rowan trees are regarded as protective and were often planted outside houses. Some Scottish families still uphold the tradition of burning a twig from a rowan tree during the Midwinter period to clear away bad feelings between family members and neighbours.

These endless Midwinter days can feel like living in perpetual twilight, but there is beauty in the gloaming too. Coming together, commemorating the past and communing with nature are all glimmers that can offer solace during the darkest days and that we can take gently into the new year.

Stories from Folklore

As the days got darker, colder weather came in and snow started to cover mountains and hilltops, our ancestors would often look to the supernatural to explain the turn of the seasons. The Celts in Scotland, Wales and the Isle of Man believed that the winter was brought about by Cailleach (pronounced 'kai-yach'), the divine hag. In Scotland, she is called Cailleach Bheurra, or Beira, the Queen of Winter who ruled the land between Samhain at the end of October, and Beltane at the start of May, while summer goddess Brìghde (pronounced 'bree-deh') was said to rule between Beltane and Samhain. In some stories, she is believed to be the same goddess with two faces. Some people believe Cailleach is the mother of all the goddesses and gods in Celtic folklore.

Cailleach is described in stories as a giant – an older woman with long, snow white hair – who would tower over the land. In many tales she is depicted as an incredibly frightening figure, sometimes with blue skin, sometimes with one eye, sometimes with copper teeth. She is said to rule from her throne on Ben Nevis, Scotland's highest mountain, surveying the lands over the winter months from her vantage point, ready to defend them. In several stories she is depicted herding deer, keeping wolves safe over winter and caring for the natural world.

One of Cailleach's most notable physical features in stories is her stature, the source of her power and strength that shaped Scotland's landscape and caused storms as she was able to summon snow and control the winds. In some versions of Cailleach's folklore, Scotland's mountains and hills are said to have been created when she strode across the land and dropped rocks from inside her creel, a type of wicker basket. In other versions of the story, Cailleach creates the mountains intentionally with her hammer, making stepping stones as she traversed the land. She is also said to have created Loch Awe, the longest freshwater loch in Scotland: tired after a long day of hunting, she fell asleep on the top of the mountain Ben Cruachan and a well there overflowed, forming a river, then a loch that flooded the valley.

In the seas, Cailleach's legacy of storms is noted by the name Corryvreckan, a strait between Jura and Scarba on the west coast that is the site of one of the largest whirlpools in the world. Corryvreckan means 'Cauldron of the Plaid', so named as Cailleach was believed to partake in a three-day ritual to clean her tartan cape before draping it, now white, over the mountain tops to dry, which caused devastatingly choppy, whirling seas and the land to become covered in snow.

As a force of nature, she was also feared; her never-ending battle with Brìghde a reminder of the perils of living off the land. In one of the most famous stories, she is depicted as jealous and cruel, punishing young, beautiful goddess Brìghde, who she captured and imprisoned in Ben Nevis because her son Angus, the King of Summer, had fallen in love with her. She set Brìghde impossible tasks, such as instructing her to wash a brown fleece white. Angus sought counsel from the King of the Green Isle, who advised him to bide his time until the Queen's reign was over when the first flowers blossomed.

One day, an old man, Father Winter, took pity on Brìghde, turned her fleece white and offered her a bunch of snowdrops to bring to Cailleach. Realising her power was beginning to wane, Cailleach sent her servants riding all over the country to defend winter but even Cailleach was no match for the turn of the seasons. Angus cast a spell on the sea and land to borrow some days from summer, causing the flowers to bloom, and nature to continue to awaken. Angus then fought with his mother, who summoned the last of the winter storms to try and drive her son from the land, causing great suffering to the people.

Angus persisted in his search for Brìghde and eventually he met her near the castle where she was imprisoned. Nature blossomed and the sun shone while the two shared their dreams and sorrows. They wed on this day – Brìghde's Day or Imbolc, the beginning of spring – and the Queen of the Fairies herself transformed Brìghde with a gown of white and silver.

Greatly angered, Cailleach drove Brìghde and Angus away to the Green Isle with her storms, where they had to wait for many years for Cailleach to lose her strength fully. During one last fight between mother and son, Cailleach – sensing the loss of her powers – is said to have fallen into a deep sleep or turned herself into a stone, depending on who you ask. She remains this way until Samhain every year, when she awakens and kidnaps Brìghde, beginning her reign of winter terror afresh. Poor Angus must fight his mother and rescue Brìghde every winter. Depending on local lore and weather, the arrival of Brìghde is still celebrated between Imbolc (at the start of February) at the earliest, and Beltane (at the start of May) at the latest.

The prominence of Cailleach persists to this day, with many place names around the west coast and across the Highlands and Islands showing how deeply she was, and still is, revered. In Highland Perthshire's Glen Lyon, there is even a shrine to the goddess, Glen Cailleach – thought to be the only surviving such shrine in the UK. Here, locals uphold the tradition of walking up Glen Cailleach on Samhain and placing symbolic stones in the shrine, representing the goddess and her family returning for winter. Local stories say that Cailleach and her family were given shelter in the glen, which flourished and became prosperous. When they left, they instructed the locals to place the stones in the shelter at Samhain, so it would continue to thrive. It has done so; called the 'longest, loneliest and loveliest glen in Scotland' according to Sir Walter Scott, Glen Lyon is part of the Loch Rannoch and Glen Lyon National Scenic Area, designated as such for its outstanding natural beauty and protected status.

Those that believe Cailleach is one face of the two-faced seasonal deity believe that on the longest night of the year she drinks magic water from the Well of Youth and starts to grow younger, and the Queen of Winter begins to relax her grip. The burning of a Yule log comes from the tradition of carving the likeness of Cailleach into wooden logs and setting them alight in the hope of banishing her and the dark troubles that she represents, as well as bringing in the literal and symbolic light.

Finding Light

Natural Woodland Decorations

An important Celtic tradition during Midwinter celebrations was to forage for evergreen foliage, bringing it inside as a symbol of everlasting life in the darkness. The ritual of seeking out and gathering greenery and berries has a deep spiritual meaning, with each of the materials gathered serving a different symbolic purpose. Holly is considered to be lucky, and in the form of a wreath represents friendship and loyalty, while ivy symbolises immortality and rebirth. Mistletoe is particularly revered in the Celtic tradition for its protective qualities – people believed it would prevent spirits of the night from entering the home. Most famously, though, mistletoe symbolises fertility, hence the tradition of kissing under the mistletoe at Christmas.

Evergreens are hung around doors and windows to protect against the darkness and getting outside to forage for my festive decor ingredients is one way that I find the light in the lead-up to Midwinter.

As well as their symbolic meanings, I love the natural and rustic feel that such materials lend to seasonal decorating, and the fact that they are sustainable, as long as they are gathered responsibly. Knowing what we do about the damage that can be done by glitter and other single-use disposable Christmas decor, we should all be looking for ways to make our decorations friendlier to the planet. If you store and look after these natural woodland decorations, they should last for many years to come – and they are fully compostable and will biodegrade once they're no longer useable, as long as you make them with natural jute, twine or raffia.

If you have a space of your own in which to grow, then you could even plan your planting with your festive decorations in mind – crab apples and Chinese lanterns (*Physalis alkekengi*) look especially festive.

'The ritual of seeking out and gathering greenery and berries has a deep spiritual meaning.'

Make it Mindful

An afternoon spent foraging in the hedgerows, field edges, woods or your garden (if you're lucky enough to have one) is a mindful way to reconnect with nature in the cold, dark months. Half the fun is spotting the beautiful shapes, colours and textures of nature and imagining how to transform them into decorations. Slowing down and engaging all our senses to really focus on the sights, sounds and feelings in our environment lets us become more attuned with our surroundings and truly appreciate them. Here are some ways to weave mindful practice into your winter crafting rituals:

- Don't wait for the weekend: try to carve out time on your lunchbreak or at the end of the day to get outside – immersing ourselves in the nature around us, no matter where we are, can be deeply grounding.
- Embed nature mindfulness in your everyday: on your walk to work, try to note down three beautiful or fascinating things in nature that you pass. You could even look for windfalls or forage in the hedgerow or public park on your way home.
- Search for a specific colour: see how many different reds you can spot in the environment around you and collect some samples to take home and decorate with. Training your eye to look for something specific is a way of engaging your brain to really see – and is even used as a strategy for averting anxiety attacks.
- Engage all your senses in the act of noticing: close your eyes and listen. What sounds can you hear? What can you feel underfoot? Is there a scent in the air?
- Look below your feet: winter storms bring nuts, berries and seedheads off branches and bushes, ideal for crafting with.
- Get outside whatever the weather: wrap up warm, wear waterproof clothing and pack a flask and a hot water bottle to make the most of unpredictable winter weather by facing the elements head on – the satisfaction of being able to cosy up again at home afterwards is hard to beat.

Materials to Collect and Their Meanings

Remember to forage responsibly and with permission. Take sparingly, no more than you intend to use. Make sure you only collect from populations that are plentiful, don't pick anything rare, and leave enough for nature to thrive. Ensure you always know what you are picking! Here are some natural materials you can look out for in nature at this time of year:

Pinecones
From the giant cones of the Coulter pine to the miniature clusters on branches of larch, choose your size depending on the craft you have in mind. Pinecones were a powerful ancient symbol, representing fertility, regeneration and enlightenment in the Celtic tradition.

Acorns
Look out for the acorns still inside their cups to help you attach them to crafts. Young acorns are green in colour and mature to a light brown. In Celtic folklore, acorns were a symbol of immortality, luck and strength, as well as wisdom and enlightenment.

Beech Nuts

If you collect them in their cases, the nut will emerge as you dry them out, but we're more interested in their spiky exterior, which can be strung up more easily. Beech trees were thought to have medicinal qualities, and they are linked with wisdom and knowledge.

Hawthorn Berries

Add a festive splash of red to decorations with clusters of berries from the hawthorn, one of the most sacred trees in Celtic mythology, representing love, protection, fertility and fairy magic. Watch out for their sharp thorns.

Honesty Seed Heads

Removing the papery outer shells of honesty seed heads reveals a translucent disk below (look out for the white or purple flowers in summer!). Honesty is also known as lunaria, meaning 'moonlike' in Latin. The moon has huge significance in Celtic culture, informing the lunar calendar and being related to success and feminine power.

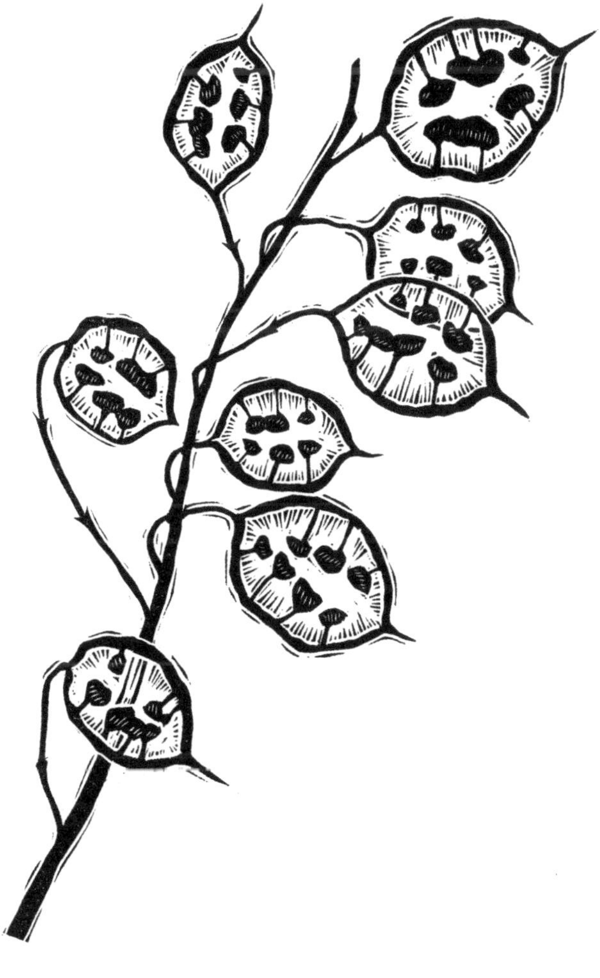

Natural Wall Hanging

We don't all have space for a tree, but a natural wall hanging is a great way of introducing foraged, festive materials to your space while taking up minimal room – it would also look lovely suspended above a celebratory table. If you can't get out to forage, then use what you have at home such as cinnamon sticks, star anise or dried orange, apple or pear slices. Natural baubles (see tip) are an even simpler variation of the craft, perfect to hang on your tree, decorate door handles, garlands or swags or to add a simple decorative touch to last minute gift wrapping too.

You will need:

- Foraged foliage or other natural festive ingredients, such as individual leaves, seedheads, acorns and pinecones, or cinnamon sticks, star anise or dried orange slices
- Twine or string
- Scissors
- A straight stick in a vsize to fit the space

First, lay out your materials – you might want to cover your surface with newspaper to avoid mess.

Decide how big you want to make your wall hanging by looking at the space you want to hang it. Think about how many strands you want your wall hanging to have and how long you want them to be – odd numbers look lovely, so three, five or seven pieces of twine spaced 10cm apart – and then cut your pieces of twine to the length you want.

Lay out your natural ingredients to decide your design, alternating different materials evenly along the lengths of the twine every 10cm or so. Then simply tie them onto the twine securely with a knot.

Attach each piece of twine to your stick at equal intervals along its length, leaving a little space at either end.

Tie another piece of twine to both ends of the stick to hang it, making a triangle shape.

Place your natural wall hanging in your desired location – as well as keeping it a safe distance away from fire and candles, it's a good idea to avoid draughts and direct light if you want it to last.

Tip

— To make natural baubles, simply cut a piece of twine or ribbon, tie the foliage directly onto it with a knot, then make another knot or bow at the end. These decorations make a lovely gift using special ribbon to make up a little set and can be kept for years as long as they're not too delicate.

Slow Gifting

Another favourite, slow Midwinter tradition of mine is making my own festive gifts. Crafting my own cards and presents when I was growing up was a highly anticipated seasonal ritual, although I think (hope!) the quality of my output has improved considerably since then. What were once handmade cards, rustic crafts and foraged nature mementos such as shells collected on walks are now handmade decorations, peppermint creams or citrus truffles.

The slow ritual of engaging all the senses in the act of making is so therapeutic to me, and has helped to centre me during many a dark winter, especially in the hectic rush in the build up to Christmas Day. In the past, making your own gifts was much more common, and this link back to my ancestors is also comforting to me. It's usually around the solstice that I set aside an evening or two to make my gifts so they're as fresh as possible for passing on, and I can always tell by the quality of the outcome if I've rushed. When the world is encouraging us to run around the shops, panic buying gifts, this time is also a gift to myself.

Peppermint Creams

The association of peppermint with the festive season has been linked to the introduction of candy canes in Germany as early as the seventeenth century. I remember my Mum making peppermint creams at Christmas, dipped in chocolate and covered in hundreds and thousands, and I've adapted her recipe here. They're easy to make but even easier to eat.

Makes approx. 60

- 225g icing sugar, plus extra for dusting
- 50g unsalted butter
- 2 tsp natural peppermint extract
- 50g milk chocolate, broken into small pieces

Sift the icing sugar into a large bowl.

Melt the butter in a small, heatproof bowl in short bursts in the microwave or in a pan over a low heat.

Once melted, add the peppermint extract to the butter and stir to combine.

Add the melted butter mixture to the icing sugar a little at a time, stirring between each addition until the mixture starts to come together into a ball.

Remove from the bowl and knead the mixture for a few minutes with your hands on a surface covered with a little icing sugar until it feels smooth. Add a little more icing sugar if you feel the mixture is too sticky.

Return the mixture to the bowl, cover and place the mixture in the fridge for 15 minutes to firm up.

Sprinkle more icing sugar on your surface and roll out the mixture to around 5mm thick.

Line a baking tray with greaseproof paper. Use a 3cm cutter to cut out small shapes (such as stars) and place them on the tray. Re-roll the scraps and continue cutting shapes out until it is all used up.

Put the tray in the fridge for an hour or so to allow the peppermint creams to firm up.

Melt the chocolate in a heatproof bowl over a pan of simmering water or in short blasts in the microwave until it just starts to melt. Leave it in the bowl for a few minutes to allow the residual heat to melt the rest of the chocolate, then stir until it is smooth.

Dip half of each peppermint cream into the melted chocolate then place them on a wire rack to set. Store the peppermint creams in the fridge – they will last for a few days.

Clementine and Star Anise Truffles

Making your own chocolate truffles takes just three ingredients – cream, chocolate and cocoa powder – but they are far more than the sum of their parts, especially if you add in some citrus zest and spice. Buy the best quality of chocolate that you can, then customise your truffle flavour with the recipient's favourite ingredients.

I like to use clementine and ground star anise in my truffles. The warming aroma from the spice beautifully enhances the zesty clementine flavour, but feel free to adapt these with your favourite citrus or spice to taste. You can easily scale up this recipe to make more truffles for multiple gifts too.

Makes 20

100ml double cream
Finely grated zest of 2 clementines
½ tsp ground star anise
200g milk chocolate, chopped into small pieces
Approx. 1 tbsp cocoa powder, for rolling

Pour your cream into a small pan and add the clementine zest and star anise.

Heat the cream gently until just shy of the boil – it should have wee bubbles around the edge.

Take the pan off the heat and add the chocolate. Leave it for a few minutes to let the heat start to melt the chocolate, then stir until completely melted with no lumps.

Chill the mixture in the fridge until it sets firm – this can take a few hours.

Place your cocoa powder in a small, flat dish. Use a spoon to scoop out 20 pieces of the truffle mixture, roughly 15g each, rolling each piece into a ball using your hands (if the mixture starts to get too sticky, refrigerate it again to firm up), then rolling each truffle in a generous coating of cocoa powder as you go and setting them aside on a plate.

Pop the truffles in the fridge to set again, and store there until ready to gift.

Tip

— The truffles will keep for a few days in the fridge, or you can freeze them individually. Remove from the freezer and defrost overnight in the fridge.

Forcing Paperwhites

Whether foraging evergreens in the woods to decorate your space, collecting windfall pinecones from the park to make a garland or making a winter wreath with foliage from your local florist, bringing the outside in is a way to ground ourselves and connect with nature in the darkest days of winter. Growing or 'forcing' bulbs indoors is especially rewarding – there's something magical about spotting those first shoots, impossibly green, emerge from a pot of earth and seem to grow before your eyes when the world is so bare. Planting indoor bulbs in the lead-up to the winter solstice means they will start to emerge in the darkest days of the year when we need them the most, and they would make a wonderful gift too, perhaps planted in a vintage receptacle that the giftee can reuse in the future. I recommend getting bulbs bred for this purpose, such as paperwhites – their tiny, pure, snowy petals are the perfect palate cleanser for the bright lights of Christmas. Plant them a few weeks apart to keep the flowers coming in succession all winter.

You will need:

A tall receptacle – any pot, vase, glass or vessel with a narrow neck to keep the bulbs in place above the level of the water
Gravel or stones
Paperwhite (narcissi) bulbs for indoor planting
Twigs (optional)
Twine (optional)

Take your receptacle and place some gravel or stones in the base for drainage and to rest the bulbs on.

Place the bulbs close together on top of the gravel or stones, pointed side up, so that they're almost touching, then add a little more gravel on top to ground them.

Add water to the receptacle, making sure the roots are underwater but the bulbs are just above the surface – the roots will get enough water to suit the needs of the plant, but if the bulb is sitting in water it will rot.

For the first two weeks, keep the bulbs in a cool, dark place (around 10–15°C), making sure their water is topped up as necessary. This is so the roots develop.

After two weeks, move them to a warmer, sunnier area, such as a sunny windowsill, and watch for the shoots to emerge. Make sure to turn the plants regularly so they grow evenly (otherwise they will grow towards the main light source).

As the bulbs begin to flower, move them to a cooler area. Deadhead any that go over to maintain the longevity of your flowers.

If the rim of your vessel is on the lower side and your paperwhites start to flop as they grow taller, you can stake the shoots with twigs by placing them carefully in the gravel or stones (without disturbing the roots) and tying the stems to the twigs with a little twine.

Tip

— You can also plant your bulbs in compost. Put gravel in the bottom of your receptacle (making sure it has drainage holes), then fill it with 8–15cm of compost. Plant the bulbs 2.5–5cm apart with their tips slightly below the rim of the receptacle. Give them a good water. Follow the same steps as above, making sure the soil is always moist.

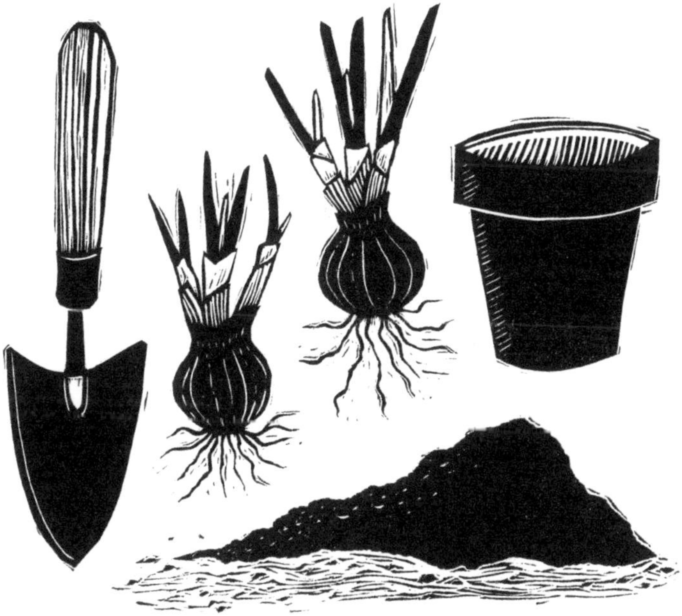

Clementine and Almond Buns

Oranges and lemons made their way to Scotland as early as the sixteenth century via the port of Leith and were sometimes even grown by wealthy people in their glasshouses or orangeries. Citrus fruits and almonds feature frequently in recipe books of the eighteenth century aimed at the upper classes, along with spices and nuts such as almonds, and the legacy of these ingredients remains today. On slow Midwinter mornings, making these clementine and almond buns is a delicious seasonal treat, the zesty fruit in the dough and icing pairing beautifully with the sweet, nutty marzipan filling. You can make the dough the night before and leave it to prove in the fridge overnight, then do the final prove and bake in the morning. A longer prove makes them taste even better.

Makes 12

For the dough:
130g plain flour, plus extra for dusting
120g strong flour
180ml whole milk
20g unsalted butter
5g salt
5g fast action dried yeast
Zest of 1 clementine

For the filling:
25g unsalted butter, softened
75g soft brown sugar
150g marzipan, grated

For the topping:
A little golden syrup, for glazing
Juice and zest of 1 clementine
100g icing sugar, or enough to make a thick water icing
20g toasted flaked almonds

First, make the dough. Combine all the dough ingredients in the bowl of a stand mixer and knead for 10 minutes. You could also do this by hand for a little longer.

Cover the dough with a damp tea towel and leave to rise for an hour, or until doubled in size. Alternatively, you can leave it in the fridge overnight to slow down the prove.

Next, make the filling. Cream the butter and sugar using a wooden spoon in a bowl and set aside. Line two 20cm round tins with baking parchment.

Lightly dust your work surface with a little flour and roll out the dough into a large rectangle approx. 20 x 30cm and about 5mm thick. Spread the filling over the surface in an even layer, then sprinkle with the grated marzipan.

Starting with the long end, roll the dough into a tight spiral, pressing the edges together to seal it. Chop the dough into 12 rounds, approx. 3cm thick, and place 6 inside each tin. Make sure you space them a little apart as they will grow as they prove.

Prove for at least half an hour, covered with a damp tea towel, until roughly double in size again. Meanwhile, preheat the oven to 190°C/Fan 170°C/Gas Mark 5.

Bake the buns for 25–30 minutes, until golden brown. Remove them from the oven. While the buns are still warm, glaze them with a little warmed golden syrup for added shine and stickiness.

While the buns cool a little in their tins, make a thick icing by mixing half the clementine zest with the icing sugar, then add a little of the clementine juice at a time until it has a consistency that coats the back of a spoon, then drizzle the icing over the top of the buns.

Sprinkle the top with toasted almonds and the remaining clementine zest and serve warm from the tins.

Embracing Darkness

Wreath Folklore

Wreath-making is a tradition rooted in seasonal symbolism, representing the cycle of nature, interconnection and everlasting life. They are especially associated with Midwinter and are usually made with evergreen foliage to symbolise enduring life in the darkness and hope for the spring to come. Wreaths were often used in conjunction with candles in various rituals of the season, honouring the darkness while signifying faith in the turn of the year and future abundance. What's more, making a wreath is a ritual in itself – gathering greenery, mindfully arranging evergreens and thoughtfully crafting them into a decoration. Making something beautiful from such scarcity is an important reminder of the resilience of nature and of ourselves in winter, and I tend to keep my wreath up until Imbolc for this reason.

If you have access to a green space of your own, then offcuts from pruning will be enough, or trimmings from your Christmas tree or from tree sellers or garden centres also work and are a thrifty option! If you are foraging, remember to get the landowner's permission and to take sparingly from each plant or tree, cutting no more than you need.

Making a Miniature Wreath

This is a miniature, 10cm version of a Midwinter wreath that is quick, cheap and easy to make, and can be used to decorate inside the house or adorn gifts. You could also scale this up into a full-sized wreath by using a willow or grape vine wreath base sourced from a florist and following the same steps using bundles of foliage made from three pieces of hand-sized greenery. Most evergreens dry out beautifully, but if you want to freshen up your wreath then you can spritz it with a little water or remove and replace any tired looking evergreens.

You will need:

Evergreens (Cyprus works well as a little goes a long way)
Florist's wire
Florist snips or heavy-duty scissors
Ribbon
Twine (optional)

Decide on the size of circle you want to make, then make your wire base by creating a circle out of florist's wire in your desired diameter, then wrap the wire twice more around the circle, weaving it round and round to create a sturdy base.

Prepare your greenery by snipping it into small sprigs.

Add your greenery to your wreath base by placing your first sprig of greenery in position and securing the stem to your wreath base with florist's wire by wrapping it around several times as tightly as you can.

Keeping the wire attached to the wreath, place your next sprig of greenery on top, overlapping the binding point of the last sprig, and secure it in place by wrapping the wire around again several times.

Continue adding your greenery in the same direction and wiring it securely to your wreath until the entire wreath base is covered.

Wrap the wire round to the back of the wreath and cut it, then tuck it neatly into the greenery to hide it. If there are any places that look a little sparse, you can wire in further pieces of greenery where there are gaps. If there are any pieces that are a bit unruly you could trim them off, but I think it's better when wreaths don't look perfect and have a more rustic movement and asymmetry.

Measure a length of ribbon the size you want your bow to be and cut it, then tie it into a bow and attach it with another piece of wire looped through the back of the knot.

Hang your mini wreath with another piece of ribbon or twine, cut to the length you want it to hang at.

Frangipane Mince Pies

Baking Yule bread is a tradition that originates in the Shetland and Orkney Isles, where families would make a plaited loaf in the shape of a circle to represent the sun. Caraway seeds are baked into the bread, thought to ward off the Sìdhe (pronounced 'shee') or spirits of winter, and some families would hide a trinket for luck inside the bread, much like the tradition of concealing a coin in the Christmas pudding. The dried fruit, spices and nuts of Yule bread have much in common with other festive recipes, such as mince pies.

I have fond memories of baking mince pies with my gran and mum, who always topped them with a simple festive star of pastry. These days, I like to add an almond frangipane topping, which brings an extra nutty sweetness that seems to absorb the mincemeat spice. This recipe makes much more frangipane than you need but sadly you can't halve an egg! (See the note below for storage tips.) This is a lovely longer bake for slow festive weekends, but you can use shop-bought shortcrust pastry if you don't fancy making your own. Buy the best mincemeat you can, perhaps from a local bakery or grocer.

Makes 12
110g plain flour
15g caster sugar
50g cold, unsalted butter, cut into small cubes, plus more for greasing
250g mincemeat
Icing sugar, for dusting (optional)

For the frangipane:
120g unsalted butter, at room temperature (bring out 30 minutes before you need it)
120g caster sugar
1 large free-range egg
120g ground almonds
Finely grated zest of 1 clementine

First, make your pastry. Mix the flour and sugar together in a large bowl and rub in the butter lightly with your fingertips – or whizz together briefly in a food processor – until the texture is like coarse sand.

Add 1 tablespoon of water to the pastry mixture and use a knife to cut and stir, bringing your crumbs together into a dough, then pat it together gently with your hands. Alternatively, blitz again briefly in the food processor. If the dough doesn't come together, add a little more water. Be careful not to over-process, or your pastry will be tough.

Cover the pastry and pop it in the fridge for around 30 minutes to rest.

On a lightly floured surface, roll the dough out thinly to 2–3mm thick, then cut out circles with a cutter slightly bigger than the holes in your 12-hole pastry tin.

Grease each of the holes in the tin lightly with a little butter then line them with the pastry circles, pressing them in gently with your fingertips.

Refrigerate for 15 minutes or so while you make your frangipane. Preheat the oven to 220°C/Fan 200°C/Gas Mark 7.

Cream the butter and sugar in a bowl with a wooden spoon until well combined, then add the egg, ground almonds and clementine zest. Mix until just combined.

Remove your pastry tin from the fridge and fill each of the pastry cases with a generous teaspoon of mincemeat.

Top each of the mince pies with two teaspoons of frangipane. Don't worry if there are wee bits of mincemeat fruit showing, it will bubble out and make a lovely fruity, sticky bit of yumminess.

Bake in the preheated oven for 12–15 minutes until the pastry and topping are golden brown.

Allow the mince pies to cool in the tin until you can handle them, then remove from the tin and let cool on a wire rack. Best enjoyed warm, sprinkled with icing sugar and with your favourite topping – rum butter or clotted cream – and a pot of tea.

Tip

– The leftover frangipane keeps in the fridge for a week, and in the freezer for a month. Roll it into a sausage shape and cut slices as needed to fill and top past-their-best croissants, then bake until golden for twice-baked almond croissants.

Chocolate and Chestnut Yule Log

On the winter solstice at dusk, a large Yule log was traditionally brought into the house and lit to represent the symbolic conquering of darkness and to ward off evil spirits. As part of this annual ritual, the fire is meant to be lit by the remnants of the previous year's log, which are kept especially for this purpose, and for luck throughout the year. Once lit, the Yule log was supposedly not allowed to go out by itself for twelve days – the length of time the Celts believed the sun stood still in the middle of winter – before being deliberately extinguished, and part of the log saved for the next year.

There's deep comfort in the idea of this ritual, I think: the Yule log's symbolic light and warmth being transmuted from one year to the next.

Today, as well as lighting fires in the hearth as a nod to the Yule log (though I do know some families who maintain the tradition of saving part of the log for the next year) people are more likely to be found tucking into a chocolate Yule log – a chocolate Swiss roll cake, decorated to look like a branch. The ritual of baking the cake, shaping and decorating it before enjoying it together is symbolic of the Yule logs of the past, and a tasty way to ward off the darkness. Make sure you enjoy it with good company, light the fire or plenty of candles and drink a glass or a mug of something warming alongside your celebratory cake. In my recipe, I also nod to the tradition of foraging for nuts and berries during Midwinter, incorporating festive chestnuts into my Yule log for extra rich flavour and symbolic magic.

Serves 10–12

For the cake:
4 large free-range eggs
100g caster sugar
60g self-raising flour
40g cocoa powder

For the filling:
150ml double cream
2 tsp vanilla extract

For the ganache:
225g double cream
200g milk chocolate, cut into small squares
200g chestnut purée

Start by making the ganache: heat the double cream in a large bowl set over a small pan of simmering water until just starting to bubble. Add the milk chocolate and remove from the heat to let the residual heat melt it.

Once melted, stir until the mixture is glossy, then add the chestnut purée and stir until fully combined with as few lumps as possible. It will start to look thicker. Transfer the mixture to a shallow dish in the fridge to firm up for several hours.

Preheat the oven to 200°C/Fan 180°C/Gas Mark 6. Lightly grease a 20 x 32cm Swiss roll tin and line it with baking parchment, pushing it right into the corners.

Next, make the cake. Either in a stand mixer with the whisk attachment or with an electric whisk, whisk the eggs and sugar together until light, pale and frothy – the mixture should increase significantly in volume and will take about 10 minutes to get to this stage.

Sift the flour and cocoa powder over the egg and sugar mixture, then gently fold it through with a metal spoon until fully incorporated with no lumps.

Pour the mixture into the prepared tin and spread it out evenly, all the way into the corners. Bake for 8–10 minutes until the edges begin to shrink from the tin and the middle bounces back in response to being lightly pressed. The cake will look light and bubbly.

While the cake is still hot, place a piece of baking parchment bigger than your cake onto a work surface and gently invert the cake onto the paper. Carefully remove the original lining paper (which will now be on the top).

Trim the edges of the cake with a sharp knife (any bits you cut off are a chef's perk!) and, being careful not to cut all the way through, make a score mark 2.5cm in from the edge along a long side – this will help your roll to get started.

Starting with this longer edge, roll the cake up so that the paper is now spiralled inside and set aside to cool completely.

Meanwhile, make the filling: whip the double cream with the vanilla extract until it forms soft peaks.

Continues overleaf

Unfurl the cold Swiss roll and remove the paper. Spread a third of the chocolate ganache over the surface until 5mm away from each edge. Spread the whipped cream on top.

Roll the cake up as before, starting with the long edge.

Slicing on the diagonal, cut off a third of the cake. Transfer the large piece of cake to a serving plate and press the other piece into the side to make it look like a branch – use more ganache if it needs a little help to stick together.

Put the remaining ganache into a piping bag fitted with a medium star nozzle. Pipe long, thick lines along the cake so that it looks like the bark of a tree. Repeat until the whole cake is covered then set aside to allow the ganache to set.

Tips

- For an easy festive dessert, you could forego making the cake and just make the ganache: set it in small, individual ramekins and top with a dollop of the vanilla whipped cream each, then decorate with a sprinkle of chocolate shavings and serve with shortbread biscuits.
- If you're not confident piping or don't have a piping bag, you can cover the cake with the ganache using a palette knife in a swooshing motion and then drag a fork down the length of the 'branches' to make a bark texture.

Upcycled Hot Water Bottle Cover

There's a cliché that Scottish people can be tight with money, but I like to think we're thrifty and great at thinking of alternative uses and extra lives for objects in our homes! This hot water bottle cover is one such make: a lovely way to repurpose a jumper you no longer reach for or to upcycle a charity shop find.

It would make a fun gift, or perhaps a gift to yourself at a tough time of year. You don't even need a sewing machine to make it (though it will be quicker if you do). A knitted rollneck is perfect for this, as the neck will become the neck of the hot water bottle – but if you only have knitwear without, you could simply roll over the top and hem it instead!

You will need:
An old jumper, preferably with a rollneck
A hot water bottle
Tailor's chalk or a fabric pen
Measuring tape
Pinking or fabric shears
Pins
A needle (or a sewing machine)
Thread in a matching colour

Wash and dry your jumper flat, then turn it inside out and place it, smoothed out, on a flat surface.

Place your hot water bottle on top of the jumper, making sure that the top of the hot water bottle is lined up with the top of the rollneck, and trace around its shape with tailor's chalk.

Remove the hot water bottle. Draw another line 1cm to the outside of your original line to give a little seam allowance.

Pin both sides of the (still back to front) jumper together along your first line to keep it together, then cut around the outside line with your pinking or fabric shears.

Sew with a straight stitch along your original line all the way around up to the neck of the hot water bottle cover so that the layers are stitched together. Make sure you leave the neck open!

Trim the seam allowance then turn the fabric the right way out, fold the hot water bottle and insert it through the neck of the cover.

Tip

— You can personalise your hot water bottle with embroidery, buttons or ribbons in contrasting or complementary colours.

Recycled Metal Decorations

In the past, Yule celebrations were far thriftier: folks would use what they had and turn simple, plain, everyday objects into beautiful decorations. A few years ago, I did an online workshop with artist Jess Wheeler where we made decorations out of old tubes of tomato purée, which sounds like it shouldn't work but is incredibly effective! The inside of a tomato purée tube is aluminium, usually gold in colour. You can then flatten out the metal and cut it into shapes, before using a pencil or old pen to emboss patterns. Simple shapes such as leaves work well, but let your imagination run free. If you're making these with children, watch out for sharp edges!

You will need:
A piece of card
Pencil (not sharp but not blunt) or dried up ballpoint pen
Scissors
An empty tube of tomato purée, cut open and washed, or a sheet of embossing metal (you can get this online or from craft shops)
Teaspoon

First, make a template for your design on a piece of card. You can do this freehand and draw your shape, trace around an object or image or use a cookie cutter as a guide. Cut around the piece of card to make your stencil.

Flatten and smooth out the tomato purée tube with the back of a teaspoon. Place your stencil on top of the back of the metal sheet (which will have the tomato purée branding on) as close to the edge of the metal as you can (you want to maximise the number of shapes you can get out of the tube). Pressing firmly, use your pencil or pen to draw round the template to create your shape.

Cut around the shape. For a smooth line, try to do this in as few fluid movements as possible.

Use your spoon to smooth out the metal again – press down firmly with the back of the spoon, pushing it outwards gently all over and all the way round your shape.

Now you can add embossed patterns and details to your design using your pencil or pen, again on the back of the tube. You could add a border following the outline or add detail to your design. For example, if you have cut a leaf shape you could add veins to it with simple lines.

Tip

— To hang your decoration, make a hole with a hand punch designed for metal, or a craft knife and cutting mat, before embossing.

Paper Bag Stars

Some people believe that the practice of decorating pine trees came from the solstice tradition of adorning evergreen trees with colourful decorations representing the sun, moon and stars. Here, these simple, star-shaped decorations are made from paper bags, using the same principle as making cut-out snowflake decorations, so they're incredibly nostalgic – but the layers make them three dimensional too. They look lovely en masse, so repeat until your heart's content! Store your stars carefully so you can reuse them, then recycle them once they're looking a bit tired. Again, I think these are more wintery than Christmassy so I often keep my star decorations out past Hogmanay to bring seasonal cheer to dark corners at home.

You will need (for each star):

8 paper bags, roughly the same width
Scissors
Glue stick
Hole punch
Twine, string or embroidery thread

If your paper bags have handles, cut them off.

Take your first paper bag and draw an upside-down T-shaped line on the front of the bag with the glue, across the bottom then up the middle, then place the next bag on top, with the base of the bags aligning. Repeat with the rest of the bags, leaving the last one glue free on top.

Cut the top corners off the bags, cutting from the middle of the bags' sides to the middle of the top on each side (though don't worry if it's not perfectly even!). You should be left with a house shape, with a pointed roof and flat walls on each side.

Cut evenly spaced triangles into the walls of the house as big as you like (as long as it doesn't cut through the centre). The more triangles you cut, the more holes will be in your star.

Draw another upside-down T-shape onto the top bag with the glue stick, and unfold the bags to make your star, pressing the front to the back to join the two ends together.

Use a hole punch to make a hole in one of the points of the star. Thread your string through, tie in a knot or a bow and hang your star in place.

Tip

— If your bags have a gusset, you will need sharp scissors as this creates more layers.

Hogmanay Mocktails

The seasonal celebration of Hogmanay dates back to Pagan times and was part of the Midwinter festival of Yule and the so-called 'daft days' from 25 December to 'Handsel Monday' (the first Monday of the year), where hosting, food and drink were offered in a bid to appease the spirit realm. Hogmanay became the main seasonal celebration alongside the winter solstice when Christmas was banned in Scotland during the Reformation. There are many traditions associated with the holiday, most famously the singing of 'Auld Lang Syne' – written by Scottish bard Rabbie Burns – after the bells as the new year begins. It's also traditional in Scotland to clean the house on New Year's Eve, including removing ashes from the hearth – clearing out the old year to welcome in the new.

I've been teetotal for more than seven years now; luckily these days it's easier to celebrate without the booze or make Dry January a joy as there are so many alcohol-free alternatives available, from kombuchas to shrubs to alcohol-free spirits. At home, whenever I have guests, I always try to supply a creative and inclusive non-alcoholic option – so each of the below recipes can be enjoyed by non-drinkers but would also go well with a shot of your favourite tipple.

Marmalade and Ginger Fizz

Hogmanay was once known as 'Auld (Old) Year's Night' – a time to say goodbye to the old year before welcoming the new. For many, this was celebrated with fire rituals (see page 112) and a fiery 'wee dram' (or two) of whisky to toast to health, wealth and happiness. This recipe came from my desire to enjoy something similarly warming on a cold winter's night that was alcohol-free. The comforting citrus from the marmalade pairs beautifully with aromatic ginger to make a spicy citrus drink that feels cosy and celebratory without the booze. Just remember to raise your glass to say cheers with the traditional Scottish Gaelic phrase, 'slàinte mhath' (pronounced 'slanj-a-vah').

Serves 2

Juice of 2 clementines
2 tbsp marmalade
Ice cubes
300ml non-alcoholic ginger beer
Dried orange slices, to garnish (optional)

In a jug, muddle the clementine juice and marmalade until the marmalade dissolves.

Divide the marmalade mixture equally between two glasses, add ice cubes, then top up with ginger beer.

Stir to mix, then garnish with dried orange slices, if you like.

Pinecone Syrup and Apple Mocktail

Mugolio is a traditional syrup made in the Italian Alps from young, green pinecones, and is steeped for a long time. This is an alternative, made in three weeks by combining just sugar and pinecones – the moisture from the pinecones makes a syrup by dissolving the sugar over time, which then lightly ferments because of the natural yeasts on the surface of the pinecones. Use any edible pinecones, experimenting with different varieties for slightly different flavours, just make sure they are green – admittedly, this is easier in late spring and early summer, but you can freeze them when you forage them earlier in the year or buy them frozen from specialist foraging websites online. You can use the syrup as you would honey or maple syrup, or top it up with soda water to make a pine cone spritz. Citrus notes from the pine pair beautifully with apple juice in this mocktail too.

Serves 2

For the pinecone syrup:
Green pinecones, cleaned
Light soft brown sugar, as needed

For the mocktail:
2 tbsp pine cone syrup
300ml apple juice
Apple slices, to garnish

Weigh your pinecones, then measure out an equal amount of sugar.

Sterilise a jar just big enough to hold the pinecones, the sugar will fill the gaps: wash the jar in warm, soapy water then dry it in the oven at 120°C/Fan 100°C/Gas Mark ¼ for 20 minutes.

Allow to cool a little, then pour a third of the sugar into the bottom of the jar. Add half of the pinecones in a layer, then cover with another third of the sugar. Add the remaining pinecones then the final third of sugar on top. Depending on the size of your pinecones, you may want to do more layers so they are all in contact with some sugar.

Leave in a cool, dark place for three weeks. Invert the jar every few days to encourage the sugar to dissolve in the resin from the pinecones and the wild yeasts to begin the fermentation process. 'Burp' the jar by opening it every few days to release the build-up of pressure from fermenting.

Once ready, strain your syrup through a sieve lined with a muslin into a clean jar and store in the fridge – it will keep for several months.

To make an apple mocktail for two, simply add 1 tablespoon of the syrup to the bottom of each glass, then top up each with apple juice and mix with a long spoon until the syrup dissolves. Garnish with apple slices and serve.

Hedgerow Shrub

Shrubs – a type of sweet, drinking vinegar – are a great alternative to alcohol during the festive season, bringing a sharp-sweet complexity that makes for a non-alcoholic option that's a bit more interesting. By now, most hedgerow fruits are over for the year, but I tend to keep a freezer stash for this purpose, or get ahead and make mine in the late autumn when the last of the hedgerow fruit such as rosehips and sloes are still around. The flavour will depend on the mixture of fruit you use. Making a shrub with honey adds an additional, aromatic sweet note, and while shrubs are usually made with cold, macerated fruit, hedgerow fruit needs a helping hand to extract the flavour. The ratio is 1:1:1 (fruit: cider vinegar: honey), so you can scale this up or down depending on how much you want to forage!

Makes 400ml
200g hedgerow fruit, frozen
200ml apple cider vinegar
200g honey

Weigh out your frozen foraged fruit, then measure out the same weights of the apple cider vinegar and the honey.

Wash a large, round-necked jar in warm water and dry it in the oven at 120°C/Fan 100°C/Gas Mark ¼ for 20 minutes to sterilise.

Prepare the fruit by slicing it into smaller pieces to help get the juices flowing.

Cook the fruit in a large pan over a medium heat with a splash of water and simmer until the juices are running.

Remove from the heat and let it cool.

Pour the mixture into the sterilised jar, add the cider vinegar and honey and seal. Shake to begin the dissolving process.

Place the jar in a cool, dark place for a few days to allow the flavour to develop.

Once you're ready to use your shrub, strain it through a sieve lined with muslin into a sterilised, 400ml jar (using the same technique as above). Serve it diluted to your desired strength with soda water.

Store the remaining shrub in the fridge – it should keep for several months, but discard if it starts to smell bad or you spot any signs of mould.

'Coal Lump' Chocolate Marzipan Biscuits

Another Hogmanay tradition is 'first footing': visiting friends or family immediately after midnight. The very first visitor was meant to be a tall, dark-haired man for luck – a tradition that apparently dates back to Viking invasions, when the arrival of a blonde man could be bad luck (I say this coming from a family of blondes!). The stranger should come bearing gifts of a black bun (a rich fruit cake covered with pastry) and a lump of coal to ensure the house was fed and warm. These chocolate and marzipan biscuits are a much tastier way to bring luck if you ask me, and a great way of using up any leftover marzipan in your festive larder. Again, I put this recipe firmly in the winter-not-Christmas list, so enjoy them well into the new year.

Makes 12

100g unsalted butter
50g caster sugar
125g self-raising flour
25g cocoa powder
Pinch of sea salt
75g marzipan, chopped into small pieces
50g milk chocolate, chopped into small pieces
12 flaked almonds, to top (optional)
Icing sugar, to dust (optional)

Preheat the oven to 180°C/Fan 160°C/Gas Mark 4. In a stand mixer, or by hand in a big bowl with a wooden spoon, cream the butter and sugar together until light and fluffy.

Sift the flour and cocoa powder into the bowl, add the salt and mix again until the mixture starts to come together into lumps.

Add the marzipan and the chocolate pieces, mix again briefly, then use your hands to form the mixture into a dough. It will be quite crumbly in texture, but this means your biscuits will be nice and short.

Roll the dough into 12 equally sized balls, each weighing about 35g, between your hands. Place the biscuits onto a baking tray lined with parchment paper with a wee space between them, and top each with a flaked almond, if using.

Bake for 12–15 minutes until the biscuits have darkened slightly and started to firm up, then leave to cool for at least 10 minutes on the tray before moving them to a wire rack to cool completely.

Dust with icing sugar, if you like, and serve.

War

END OF JANUARY TO MID-MARCH

In spite of their proximity to spring, the ongoing darkness and cold of February and early March can actually feel the heaviest of the winter months.

The sparkle and celebration of Christmas is now a mere memory, and the novelty of a new year is overtaken by seemingly endless grey days. It's tempting to rush ahead into the next season, and as the shops begin to fill with imported flowers and premature Easter egg displays, the world seems to urge us onward, pressuring us to leave our winter nests behind and throw ourselves into spring at a time where energy may still be lacking, and motivation in short supply.

In reality, the days are still short, nights still long and weather, most often, interminably cold. Here in Scotland this is usually the harsher side of winter, rather than December, with ice and snow a common occurrence where I live. There's also a growing pressure to be productive and 'getting on with it' now that we're a few months into the year. It's a recipe for feeling disconnected and down, if you think about it.

Instead, I invite you to linger in winter a little longer. To wrap yourself in blankets, to top up that hot water bottle, to make another pot of tea and light the candles a while more. To tend to your own needs and nurture yourself into spring, instead of rushing on to the next thing.

Nature doesn't hurry. Nature knows. Nature tends to roots, shoots and buds. Look at snowdrops: they prefer the cold, they can push through the snow and the frozen earth to bloom – but they're the early ones. Their arrival marks a small but important shift towards spring, but for many flowers it's still too cold. They might be stirring quietly beneath the surface, but they are still protecting themselves from the harshest weather. When we notice our environment, we can notice our own needs, what we need to bloom. Soon – but not too soon.

In our modern world, we tend to think of spring, summer, autumn and winter as four distinct seasons, which stops us noticing the in-between spaces as winter blossoms gently into spring. It emerges bud by first bud, leaf by new leaf: a tentative unfurling. Yet this liminal time is one that I feel we need to appreciate the most: embracing rest and slowness, but also knowing that the light and life of spring is on its way.

Tentative Transitions

Here in Scotland, we have a word for this earliest period of spring: Waretym. Ware-day is the first day of spring on the 1 March, with its prefix 'ware-' even used as an adjective, 'wairie', meaning cold and bleak, as well as unproductive. Language itself tells us that spring is arriving, but gradually, maybe even seeming fruitless for a time.

Figuratively, waretym can also refer to the very start of life. This is a time for truly nurturing, for deep rest and intuitive care, for holding our inner infant and tending to their needs: swaddling them in softness, nourishing their body, caring for them like a newborn babe.

This is far easier said than done, I know: this self-compassion has taken me a long time to develop and is still something I need to consciously practise, especially in the cold, dark season. I used to share my year in review posts on social media and cheerily wish colleagues a happy new year, then struggle on through January like many of us do. By the time February and March rolled around, winter dragging its heels, I would feel I had no real reason to be depressed any more, attempt to bury the intrusive thoughts and try to push through. I now know, if anything, this made things worse.

My winter pregnancy exacerbated these feelings for me. The darkness of January was over, and I was well into the second trimester now; I should feel better. Instead, I still felt sick for most of the day, every day. The riskiest part of pregnancy had apparently passed; I should be announcing our news. Instead, I waited with bated breath for our twenty-week scan. The days still seemed an endless grey, a blur of nausea and crushing anxiety.

And then a sudden bleed and terrifying trip to obstetric triage seemed to confirm to me that things were all too precarious. On returning home after our hospital visit, constant fear and hypervigilance became entrenched in my day to day. As February arrived, my world seemed darker than ever.

A sign of how well I am, or otherwise, is how much creativity I allow in my life; how many photos I take is often a barometer for my emotional state. When I look back on that winter, there are hardly any photos. Photography is a way I record the everyday beauty around me and how I channel my creativity. But it had all dried up over that hard, harsh winter of pregnancy sickness and debilitating anxiety.

Shifting Seasons

In my camera roll, I can pinpoint the moment where my mindset began to shift and it was Waretym. There are pictures of the very first snowdrops spotted on my walk to work, highlighter yellow witch hazel, velvety catkins of pussy willow. Inspired by the deep-red blood oranges and sherbet-pink forced rhubarb at the greengrocer, I started baking again. I began planting seeds and watering them and believing they would grow.

The magic of Waretym contributed to a change in outlook that was vital after a winter of sickness and mental turmoil, and, finally, a diagnosis of perinatal anxiety and OCD opened the doors to NHS support. I started meeting my wonderful therapist Melanie weekly to formulate my emotionally informed birth plan, partly to talk through and process some of my anxieties, intrusive thoughts and compulsions, and partly so I could advocate for my needs throughout my perinatal care.

Winter was far from over, but I now had some tools to help me in the darkness and, slowly but surely, I began to see the light at the end of the tunnel. I could finally, tentatively, start to do more than just cope, and even began planning for when the baby arrived. I allowed myself to buy the first tiny baby clothes and wash and put them away in drawers. I could finally believe the baby was staying, was real. I was able to be present at last by noting my glimmers. They grew more numerous every day.

Outside, snowdrops gave way to the first daffodils. Catkins, shoots and buds became abundant. I saw a fox outside the window, searching for food on the street. The first bees began to look for food, enjoying the pollen of spring crocuses in my local park. The light grew, shyly at first, then one day I realised it was light after 5 p.m. The sun crept into the kitchen for what felt like the first time in months, warming my soul from the inside out. The birdsong seemed a little louder every single day. Some sparrows nested in the disused flue of the flat below; I watched them feathering their home to prepare for their babies too.

Celtic Spring

Perhaps the most significant milestone in the Celtic calendar during Waretym is Imbolc, the festival that marks the beginning of spring on the 1 February. This is the mid-point between the winter solstice and spring equinox as nature begins to stir from its hibernation. Some believe the festival was once more fluid and specifically linked to nature in the community: the first lambs taking their first steps, and the blooming of the blackthorn with its abundant white blossom, signalling the beginning of the growing season. It is a time associated with birth, hope and new life.

During that dark winter, reading about Waretym and Imbolc brought me comfort, helping me to feel that my growing baby and I were part of nature, not removed from it. Although the exact origin is unknown, some people believe that the name 'Imbolc' comes from the Old Irish meaning 'in the belly', referring to the pregnancy of ewes during this early springtime and the start of lambing season. Other theories associate Imbolc with words describing washing and cleaning – a period of symbolic cleansing for spring. As my nesting instinct kicked in, I felt this ancient spring connection back to my foremothers keenly.

There is so much beauty in the wild winter season, perhaps more so with the knowledge that spring must follow. We can be present in the here and now and hopeful for the flourishing ahead. To me, part of the comfort of living seasonally is this duality: holding the awareness that light follows dark, that new life will follow the death of the year. And in this in-between space of Waretym we can hold this knowledge: the quiet as well as the promise.

Stories from Folklore

As the harsh winter months continued, our ancestors' supplies would begin to run low. With very little growing outside, the animals for meat slaughtered already, stores becoming bare and preserves now in short supply, it's no wonder that they would look for and celebrate even the smallest signs of spring, of hope and of resilience, and turn to supernatural stories for comfort and wisdom. There is much to be learned from the tales of these communities – folks whose existence was intimately connected to the weather, to nature, to the land itself.

At this tipping point from winter to spring, the festival of Imbolc was pivotal, especially as it is thought to be linked with the rhythms of the farming season. This was a crucial moment in planning the farming year, so rituals and superstitions were abundant.

On Imbolc, Cailleach was believed to be gathering her firewood for the rest of the winter season. If the day brought sunny, warm weather, Cailleach was thought to be out and about, merrily gathering supplies to extend her visit and thus prolonging the wintertime. If the weather was dreich (dreary and poor), she had decided to stay asleep, and the winter was likely to pass sooner rather than later. Some believe that this is one of the origins of 'Groundhog Day' in America and Canada, also observed at the start of February and another indicator of spring's arrival (or not) depending on whether the groundhog can see its shadow.

As the days lengthened ever so slowly and new life stirred beneath the Earth, the Celts believed that Cailleach's power was waning and that the summer goddess Brìghde's power was growing once again. The Scots Gaelic name for the oystercatcher is 'gille-Brìghde' – servant of Brìghde – as stories say she would summon the birds and send them to guide sailors through storms. For this reason, their distinctive, high-pitched call is thought to herald the arrival of spring.

Imbolc was also known as 'Là Fhèill Brìghde' in Scots Gaelic and the festival is strongly associated with the ancient Celtic Goddess Brìghde. Saint Brigid – one of the patron saints of Ireland – also celebrates her feast day on the same day as Imbolc. As the pair share many of the same characteristics, some believe they were the same person, while others think that the Goddess' story was Christianised and later celebrated as St Brigid's Day or Candlemas on the 1 and 2 February instead.

Many of the seasonal rituals, including those still existing today, revolved around women and girls in the community and were closely associated with the home. A common Celtic custom that survives to this day, especially in Ireland, is the making of Brigid's Crosses. These were woven from straw or rushes the night before Imbolc and hung over doors and around the house at the start of February for good luck and protection from evil, spirits, fire and illness. Legend has it that St Brigid of Kildare wove a cross from rushes to explain Christianity, and the cross now appears in different shapes, some with four legs and a woven diamond centre, others with three legs and a triangle centre, both symbolising peace and protection.

Brìghde dolls were also thought to be made in Ireland and parts of Scotland from rushes or corn from the last harvest and decorated with cloth and nature finds such as shells or early spring flowers. The symbolic doll would be taken through the community from home to home by young girls dressed in white during Imbolc or on the eve of the festival. The story goes that the locals would give offerings of milk to the Brìghde doll and to the land, in the hope of bringing luck in the coming spring. Older women in the community are said to have made a wee cradle called the Bed of Brìghde, housing the sheaf doll who they would sing to in Gaelic to welcome her. They were thought to 'read' the ashes from the fire to confirm that Brìghde had visited, looking for her footprint or the mark of her wand as symbols of good luck for the season ahead.

Many families would eat a celebratory meal on the eve of Imbolc, with sowans (sour oats), dumplings or bannocks – like a flatbread made from barley or oatmeal and cooked on the 'bannock stane' (stone) or later a 'girdl' (griddle) – eaten or sometimes given as offerings to Brìghde to bring good luck. It is even thought that people would pour porridge into nearby rivers or streams as an offering to the spirits on behalf of the dead, so they would find favour in the spirit world. In Ireland, spring cleaning rituals often took place on St Brigid's Day, a symbolic clearing out and renewal. In Scotland, this was often done a little earlier, on Hogmanay – known as 'redding'. It was traditional to clean the house for good luck in the coming months (and consequently it was very bad luck to clean on New Year's Day in case you washed away your good fortune for the year ahead!).

Other customs during Waretym included visiting holy wells on the day of Imbolc: rituals included praying for good health while circling the well in a clockwise direction, and leaving offerings by neighbouring trees, such as coins or special objects. These wells were sometimes known as 'clootie wells' as 'clooties' (cloth strips) or ribbons were dipped in the holy water of the well and tied to nearby trees while the visitor prayed to the spirits in nature to heal them or make their wish come true. There are several wells associated with Brìghde in Scotland and Ireland, including the Well of Eternal Youth – a natural pool on the island of Iona in the Scottish Hebrides, thought to bring healing and renewal after it was blessed by Brìghde.

'There is much
to be learned
from the tales
of these communities
– folks whose existence
was intimately
connected to the
weather, to nature,
to the land itself.'

Finding Light

Signs of Spring

Even when it seems as though winter will never, ever end, nature is stirring beneath the earth, as plants and trees ready themselves for spring. One of the signs that nature is preparing for the new season can be found in the birch tree. In the winter, you can easily spot the year-round white, textural bark of the silver birch tree standing out in a landscape of brown and grey. These deciduous trees are commonly found in woodlands and heaths, but I see them increasingly in urban gardens too, as they grow quickly and offer beauty in all seasons.

In ancient Celtic mythology, the birch tree was a symbol of renewal and purification as well as love and fertility. It is linked to several of the festivals in the Celtic Wheel of the year, from birch bundles being used to make brooms to sweep out the spirits of the old year at Samhain, to lighting fires at Beltane.

I have been lucky enough to see a silver birch tree from my window in the last two places I have lived. In my old flat, our neighbours had one in their garden, and watching its progress through the seasons brought me much joy. The tree and the view of Arthur's Seat in the distance over the rooftops was the only nature I could see, and through the protracted winter of Covid-19, watching the small shifts as bare branches gave way to hopeful green leaves was so comforting. Now we are lucky enough to have a birch tree in our own communal garden in the heart of the city; in fact, its presence here was one of the 'signs' I took that this flat was the one for us as I was so sad to leave our old lockdown tree behind. Isn't it funny how we can become so attached to trees?

And it's easy to see why in winter. Paying close attention to birch trees can encourage you to really slow down and notice the small but significant changes as winter transforms into spring. Indeed, the birch tree is one of the first trees to come into leaf, its lithe arms begin by sprouting buds, then catkins, then smooth, small, triangular leaves. And don't forget to look down: the light canopy of birch encourages growth of numerous plants on the forest floor below, starting with tiny purple flowers of violets, star-shaped white wood anemones, sleepy white and purple wood sorrel (whose flowers close at night) and later the drooping purple bells of bluebells.

Fungi also thrive beneath birch trees from late summer all the way through to early winter, including the iconic red-and-white-spotted fly agaric, chanterelles and birch milk cap. The birch is a haven for insects and therefore birds too; woodpeckers are commonly known to nest in their trunks, though you're likely to hear one before you see it. It's no wonder our ancestors associated the birch with such power.

Birch Tree Foraging

Birch twig tea

Birch twig tea tastes nutty and aromatic. Gather young birch twigs (1–2mm thick green, bendy twigs) and cut them into small pieces around 1cm in length. Roast them on a baking tray for 15 minutes at 200°C/ Fan 180°C/Gas Mark 4. Allow to cool and store them in an airtight jar.

To brew, put a heaped teaspoon of the twig pieces per person in a pot with boiled and slightly cooled water. Brew until your desired strength – I find around 5–10 minutes is good. It is lovely with a splash of oat milk.

Birch leaves

Young birch leaves are delicious in a spring salad or used as you would parsley to top soups and stews.

Birch bark paper

Birch bark has been used as paper for thousands of years. Remove a peeling piece of bark from the trunk of a tree, wash with mild detergent and rub gently to remove any rough pieces. While damp, peel the layers apart, rinse and dry between paper towels, then place under a stack of books to flatten. Use as you would paper!

Birch tree brush

Collect a small bundle of skinny branches around 12cm long and strip off the bark by peeling it with your fingers. Trim the branches to the same length and tie them together tightly with dampened natural twine, such as jute, which will tighten as it dries. Use to sweep up crumbs on kitchen surfaces and clean areas that are tricky to reach.

Birch Sap Tapping

Sap is akin to human blood: it carries minerals, nutrients (including sugar produced by photosynthesis) and water around the tree. In winter, sap is stored in the roots of deciduous trees when they become dormant, and as the temperatures begin to rise as spring arrives, the sap of the tree begins to move up the trunk to the branches where it fuels production and opening of new buds.

Birch sap tapping is an ancient tradition and was used for medicinal purposes as it was thought to be anti-inflammatory. To our ancestors, the delicate sweetness of birch sap would have been a welcome taste of freshness. To our modern palette – now inured to sugar – the sap tastes barely sweet. Birch sap is watery with a slight sweetness, a woody, aromatic taste and a smooth and silky texture – almost like mineral water. I first tasted it when I went on a foraging course with Judith of Edinburgh Forage and Eat; we tapped trees in the Pentland Hills and she made us the most delicious nettle pancakes cooked over the fire and served with her own birch syrup. Birch sap can be fermented to make birch wine too, though I've not tried that one myself.

Birch tapping is an easy and rewarding wild drink to harvest, but there are a few things to keep in mind to do so mindfully and sustainably. Firstly, make sure that you don't tap very young trees – the trunks should be at least 30cm in diameter. Secondly, make sure to leave a gap between harvests: you should only tap the same tree once every three years to ensure it recovers. Lastly, to err on the side of caution, collect no more than 4–5 litres of sap from each tree. Remember (as with all foraging) to obtain permission from the landowner too.

Timing

Traditionally, birch sap was collected when the snow melted, but today our winters are far less snowy so this isn't a reliable timing method. It is tricky to give a hard and fast rule as to when to collect birch sap, as it can be ready any time from late February to early April, depending on where you live and the conditions each spring. Some people believe that the emergence of the first daffodils is a reliable sign for the sap rising, but a good rule of thumb is when the leaves begin to emerge on the birch tree – for me in central Scotland this is usually early March. To test if the sap is rising, you can cut off a thin twig near the end of a branch with a sharp knife and see if a teardrop emerges at the end. If it does, the sap is rising and the tree is ready to tap.

The traditional way to harvest birch sap is to make a hole in the bark of the main trunk, however unless you are harvesting a large amount, I think this low-impact method is much more appropriate, kinder to the tree and easier too. You will need to leave the bottle for several hours to collect the sap, so choose a tree that won't be disturbed, or place it somewhere discreetly.

You will need:
A pair of sharp secateurs/ foraging knife
Sterilised drink bottles to collect your sap (a reusable one is good)
Heavy duty wide masking tape

Choose your branch to tap: ideally one that is close enough to reach, and strong enough to hold the weight of the bottle.

About 10cm from the end, cut the end off the branch – it should start dripping sap.

Secure your bottle by inserting the branch into it and taping the bottle to the branch.

Leave your bottle in place for several hours and keep an eye on its progress. Depending on where you are in the sap rising window, the speed will vary – it can take from a few hours to several days, and of course it depends how much you want to harvest.

What to do with your sap

Birch sap is best consumed fresh, so drink it straight away, otherwise freeze and defrost as and when you want to use it. Some people claim it is a hangover cure but that might be to do with its hydrating, fresh qualities...

You can make a syrup from birch sap, which has a more robust flavour than maple syrup, and a caramel-y, almost savoury sweetness. However, as birch sap only has a small percentage of sugars (between 0.5 and 2%) you need to reduce it down significantly, so for every 100ml you collect you are likely to make only 1ml of syrup, if that. If you do want to make birch sap syrup then you can boil it down to reduce it – but make sure you watch the pan as it can catch easily.

Forced Rhubarb

Rhubarb has been used for medicinal purposes for thousands of years and was originally imported into medieval Europe from Asia. In the eighteenth century, rhubarb seeds were more valuable than gold, so efforts were made to introduce it to the UK. There is some dispute over who was first to grow rhubarb here, but one of the theories is that a Scot, Bruce of Kinnaird, introduced rhubarb seeds to the Royal Botanic Garden in Edinburgh in 1774. As sugar became more widely available, rhubarb began to be used in cooking and became a Scottish kitchen staple.

'Forced' rhubarb is quite literally trying to find the light: it is grown in the dark to encourage the plant to grow earlier and make sweeter, brighter, softer and longer stems that are delicious in late winter and early spring. Apparently the first forced rhubarb came about accidentally, when gardeners at London's Chelsea Physic Garden noted that some rhubarb had been mistakenly left covered over winter and had grown far earlier than its outdoor counterpart. The 'Rhubarb Triangle' in Yorkshire is now best known for the vibrant stems, harvested by hand in candlelight so as to maintain their bright colour. The neon pink stems of forced rhubarb taste almost like sherbet in their tart sweetness, and are a welcome addition to the kitchen when stores of apples and pears are running low after a long winter. Native to Siberia, China and Mongolia, rhubarb thrives in the cold and it's easy to grow yourself if you have a little space.

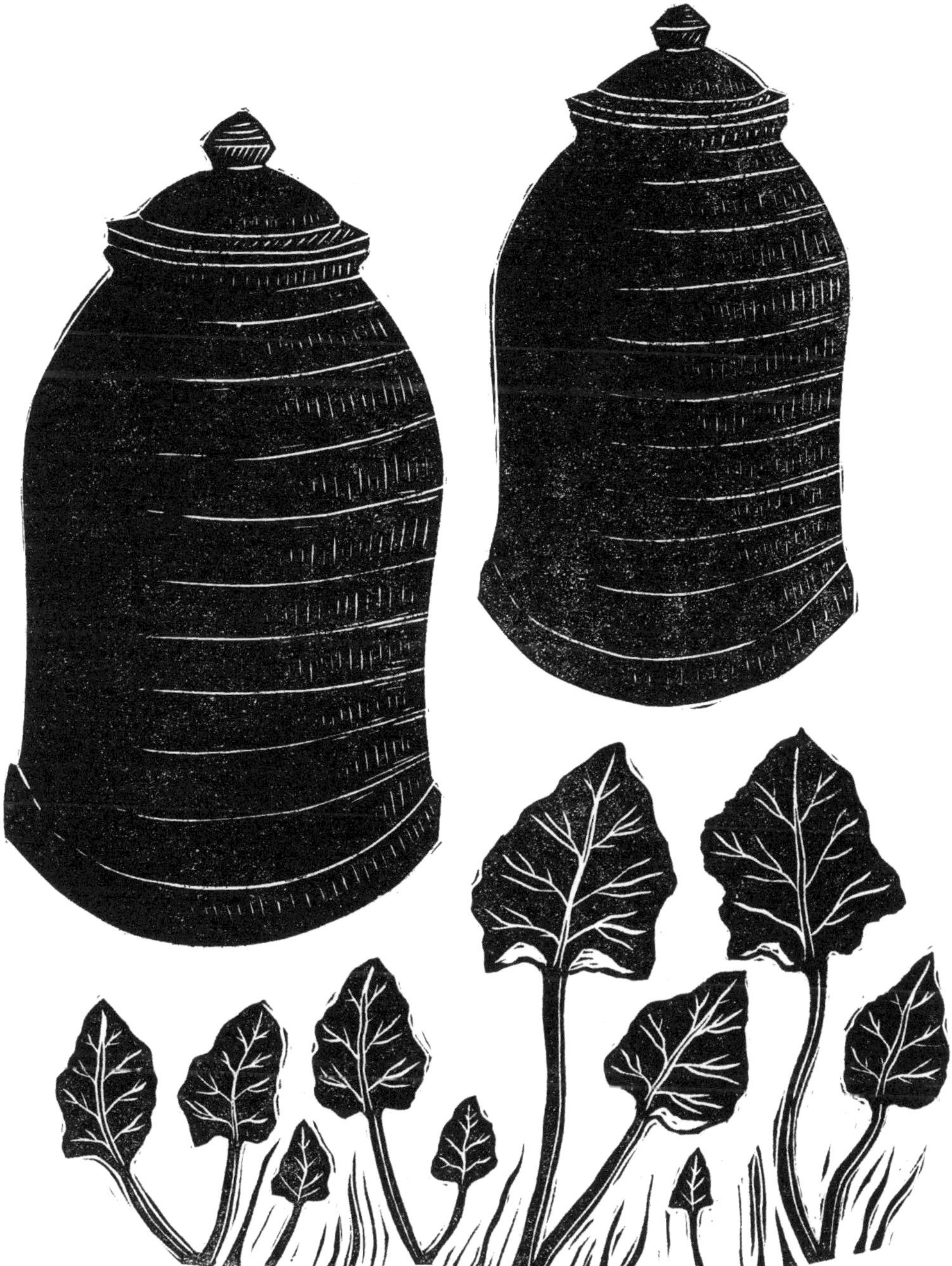

Force Your Own Rhubarb

In late winter (January) you can force your own stems of rhubarb easily by covering them up with a tall bucket or pot. We have a communal 'drying green' (a garden around the back of the tenements) so I find having a compact pot garden to be easiest and a great way to learn what will thrive and where as a total beginner gardener. If you also want to try growing rhubarb in a pot, make sure you get a compact, pot-friendly variety.

You will need:
A deep container (at least 50cm wide and deep) or a patch of the garden
Compost
A rhubarb crown (from an established rhubarb plant – choose an early cropping variety)
A tall, dark coloured bucket (at least 50cm tall)
Straw

Fill your container with compost and plant your rhubarb crown 'growing tip' up, so it is just below the top of the soil. Gently pat the soil around the crown and water it well.

Place the tall bucket over the top and make sure there are no holes that will let in the light. Insulate the outside with straw in a thick layer around the sides of the pot.

Leave to grow for 7–8 weeks. When the stalks reach the top of the pot (around 40–50cm tall) it's ready to pick by gently twisting and pulling on the stalks.

Tip

— Don't forget to water your rhubarb, especially if it's in a pot covered for forcing over winter, and then in the summer. After forcing a rhubarb plant, you should leave it to grow normally for at least the following year.

Rhubarb and Custard Cake

Rhubarb and custard is a classic combination that always makes me think of Sunday lunches at Gran and Granda's house. In fact, anything with custard was a hit with Granda. To celebrate early spring and the first stems of forced rhubarb from the greengrocer, I like to combine rhubarb and custard in a cake, where a little goes a long way: a vanilla-infused custard sponge with a custard glaze and sherbet-fresh forced rhubarb that contrasts its sweetness. Delicious with a cup of tea, or, dare I say it, warmed up with more custard!

Serves 8

- 120g unsalted butter, plus extra for greasing
- 120g soft brown sugar
- 1 tsp vanilla extract
- 2 large free-range eggs
- 120g self-raising flour
- 30g custard powder
- 120g forced rhubarb, half cut into 1cm pieces, and half cut into 7cm batons

For the glaze:

- 10g custard powder
- 10g icing sugar
- 2 tsp whole milk

Preheat the oven to 180°C/Fan 160°C/Gas Mark 4 and grease and line a 20cm round baking tin.

In a bowl, cream together the butter and sugar until light and fluffy – around 5 minutes. Stir in the vanilla extract.

Add the eggs one at a time, followed by a little flour.

Gently fold in the remaining flour and custard powder. Fold in the small pieces of rhubarb.

Pour the batter into the prepared tin, then level the surface with a spatula. Press the rhubarb batons gently into the top like the marks on a clock face.

Bake in the preheated oven for 30–35 minutes, until golden brown on top and a skewer inserted in the middle comes out clean. If the cake starts to look too brown before it is done, cover it with tinfoil.

Leave the cake to cool in the tin for a few minutes, then remove and leave to cool completely on a wire rack.

Once the cake has cooled, make the glaze by mixing the custard powder and icing sugar together, then adding the milk a little at a time until the icing is a pourable consistency, like runny honey. Drizzle over the top of the cake, then leave to set before serving.

Winter Meets Spring

Bringing the outside inside is a guaranteed way to improve my mood, even in the wintertime. In fact, the challenge of searching out beautiful things to place in a seasonal arrangement when there is so little in nature just adds to the satisfaction of making something. I often find that without the distraction of so many flowers to choose from, you can really appreciate the stark beauty of your surroundings in the cold, dark months.

And when you really slow down, really look and really engage with the outside world you can find there is a surprising amount to see and celebrate as the seasons shift – from the hardiest winter blooms to the earliest spring blossoms. I always look forward to my annual pilgrimages to Cambo Snowdrop Festival in the East Neuk of Fife, a place I've been visiting for many years, and the wonderful flowery friends I've made – and made things with – at a time of year where creativity has felt in short supply.

'There is a surprising amount to see
and celebrate as the seasons shift –
from the hardiest winter blooms to
the earliest spring blossoms.'

WHAT TO LOOK FOR:

Something Woody

Branches with Lichen or Berries

Look out for interesting-shaped branches that can add structure and shape to an arrangement. Hardier red berries such as hawthorn can still be found this side of Yule, and in the winter you can also see beautiful lichens (a hybrid of fungi and algae) adorning branches more obviously; both can add texture and unexpected colour. Search for fallen branches: soft, bushy lichens such as 'old man's beard' look almost like feathers, while common orange lichens bring a beautiful ochre yellow to muted seasonal arrangements.

Early Blossom

Peak blossom season may be a while off, but there are some early flowering varieties that you can find: cherry plum blossom has delicate white flowers, while flowering quince comes in bright shades from pillar-box red to peachy pink. Blossom doesn't last long in the vase, but you can prolong its life by placing the branches in a bucket of fresh water as soon as you cut them and leaving them for several hours to take up water.

Something Textural

Witch Hazel
When gardens are bare, the acid yellow or tangerine orange starburst petals of witch hazel add welcome brightness. A few branches of witch hazel make a stunning arrangement on their own in a simple vase, held in place with some chicken wire and a flower frog, or adding a twig or two to an arrangement will lend sculptural form and a colourful touch.

Seed Heads
Without the noise and distraction of spring and summer's riot of garden colours, textural seedheads come to the fore. There are so many wonderful shapes in nature, whether you're looking for something to make a statement (like the sculptural seedheads of alliums or the large thistles of teasels, popular with birds), something more delicate (such as the moon-like silvery coins of honesty seeds or light ornamental grasses) or something in between (such as the spiky globes of echinops or golden-brown campion seed heads).

Catkins
A sure sign that spring is on its way is the arrival of catkins, the long, slim flower clusters that grow on the branches of trees such as hazel, from January to March, and alder, in February and March. The former are long and acid yellow – often referred to as 'lambs' tails' because of their shape – while the latter are bright green. Both can bring a tactile element to arrangements.

Something Delicate

Hellebores
The drooping flowers of hellebores last all the way through winter in subtle shades of green, off-white, soft pink, plum red and purple black that seem suited to the season. They wilt easily in a vase, so for best results cut shallow slits along the stem for a few centimetres to help them absorb water, dip the end of the stem in boiling water for around 30 seconds, then condition them in a deep vase of cold water overnight before you arrange them.

Snowdrops
The green shoots and cheery white, bell-shaped flowers of snowdrops are among the first to emerge from the mud and leaf litter signalling a definite shift towards spring in their swathes on the woodland floor. Known as 'Candlemas Bells' and 'Fair maids of February', snowdrops are thought to symbolise the growing light of the winter sun. Some people think it's bad luck to bring them inside, but one or two in an arrangement as a reminder of light and new life surely can't hurt!

Narcissi

Some earlier varieties of narcissi bloom at this time of year, including the delicate, snowy white flowers of paperwhites, especially if you 'force' them indoors (planting the bulbs in the cool and dark then bringing them out into the warmth and light of your home to encourage them to grow quickly – see page 130). Their pretty white petals contrast with the dried and woodier elements in an arrangement, and they also provide a heady, spring-like fragrance.

Waretym Arrangement

Using a kenzan, pin frog or flower frog lets you create flower arrangements in different vessels without using non-biodegradable flower foam, which is damaging to the environment. Kenzans are reusable, sustainable, and perfect for single stems (like Japanese ikebana) or an arrangement like this one which uses woody stems as well as softer ones, as the weighted, waterproof pins keeps heavier stems in place, while the arrangement of the pins keeps things light and elegant.

You will need:
Branches, dried flowers or foliage, spring flowers (see pages 173–177)
A bowl
A medium-sized, round kenzan
Adhesive tack or museum wax, if you're using heavier stems (optional)
Secateurs

Gather your arrangement ingredients the day before and condition them in water overnight, removing any foliage below the water line. See the advice on pages 173–177 for flowers and foliage that need specific treatment.

The next day, lay out your flowers and branches on a table or work surface so that you can see their various shapes and colours.

Place your bowl in the middle of the table. Place the kenzan in the bottom of the bowl, attaching it to the base with adhesive tack and pressing it down firmly, if you are using heavier stems. Fill the bowl with a little water – just level with the top of the kenzan's pins.

Now the fun bit: adding the flowers! As you add them, trim each of the stems at the bottom, straight across (this will make it easier to attach to the pins). Start with your woodier elements, cutting them across and then upwards to create a small slit in the stem. Use both hands to press each stem firmly onto the pins to hold them in place.

Use the different shapes to inspire the placement of each stem, thinking about how the plant appears in nature – for example, you might want to place a beautiful curving branch to one side as though it was still attached to the trunk. Turn the vessel as you go, making sure that you're not too focussed on the front of the arrangement.

Once you can see the backbone of the arrangement emerging, add your more delicate dried elements, slotting them in between the branches to fill the gaps, thinking about using a range of different heights, shapes and textures. You might want to press heavier dried elements right into the kenzan, others will be held in place between the other stems. Remember to keep turning your arrangement as you add elements.

Lastly, add your fresh flowers, starting with the hardier stems then progressing to the most delicate so that they don't get crushed. Make sure they are in the water, again pressing into the kenzan where needed, or use the arrangement itself to hold them into place.

Tip

— If you are using a large, very open bowl, you can use a ball of chicken wire low down in the bottom of the bowl to help support the stems. Again, this can be reused and is far more sustainable than flower foam.

Woven Willow Bird Feeder

In earliest spring, one of the loveliest glimmers of joy in nature is surely the growing sound of birdsong at dawn and dusk as common garden birds such as robins, blackbirds and thrushes are singing to attract mates, their song peaking around the end of March. With food still in short supply, feeding your local birds is a great way to support our avian neighbours.

A woven willow bird feeder is both a beautiful and practical make at this time of year. Weaving with willow has been practised for thousands of years and feels all the more apt as the branches are bare and we head into spring, not to mention reminiscent of Brigid's Crosses and the Brìghde Doll. Make sure you use dried willow to craft with, otherwise your creation will shrink as it dries out. I learnt a trick for holding the willow using a bottle from local basket weaver Katie Warner – I love that you don't need any fancy kit, but can simply reuse household objects. You can source willow from local basket weavers, as well as online.

You will need:

Dried willow rods (to make a small bird feeder you will need 7 'base branches' of willow, around 50cm in length each, and several longer, slimmer branches as your 'weavers')
Water and a vessel to soak the branches in
Secateurs or pruning shears
Garden twine or string
A tall, slim glass bottle, at least 30cm tall, but as wide as your fat balls or other bird food (this is used as a kind of frame and makes it easier to hold and stop and start the craft if you need to)

First, prepare your willow: leave it to soak in water for several days. To check if the branches are ready, bend them in a gentle arc – if they bend easily and don't snap, they're suitable to work with.

Make a bundle with your seven thicker, base branches. Tie them together using the twine close to the base, roughly 2cm from the end.

Spread out your branches evenly and place them over the glass bottle with the tied base at the top.

Take one of your longer weaving branches and insert the tip of the more flexible, skinnier end between two of the thicker branches right at the top where they're tied together. Weave your weaving branch over and under each of the base branches until it runs out.

Add another weaving branch by overlapping it with the branch you've just finished, using the thicker butt end to start this time.

Continue to loosely weave up to the height that you want, matching tip to tip ends and butt to butt ends and leaving gaps between the woven strands so the birds can get at the food. You should be able to finish the end by just tucking it behind one of the base branches.

Remove the bird feeder from the bottle. To finish your bird feeder, bring the stems together into a bundle again and tie at the top with more string. Attach your feeder using another piece of string.

Embracing Darkness

Spring Cleaning

At this time of year, I feel the urge to spring clean. It comes upon me suddenly, like a nesting instinct, every Waretym. Simply being at home more often during the darker months can mean a bit more mess, dust and dirt, so taking time to declutter and deep clean feels like a small but important act of self-care. More deeply than that, ritual cleaning is said to have been part of traditional Imbolc celebrations, and I can certainly see the logic; a symbolic letting go of winter and welcoming in of the spring.

Citrus Cleaning Spray

I looked into making my own, eco-friendly cleaning products when thinking about having a small human in the house, and not only were they easier to make than I thought they would be, but they're also cheaper and a great way to combat household waste too. In late winter, I seem to get through a lot of citrus fruit. With food feeling all the more precious in the darker months, especially the vivid colour and flavour of oranges and lemons, I find that I don't want to waste a thing. After experimenting with making citrus powders for cooking (more than a little faff) or stashing scraps in the freezer for flavouring glasses of water throughout the year (they inevitably languished, forgotten) I tried making this citrus cleaning spray to make use of my discarded peel. It's a staple, all-purpose cleaner with a mild anti-bacterial effect and is great at cutting through grease – just bear in mind that it isn't as strong as a shop bought disinfectant.

You will need:
A small sandwich bag full of citrus peel
A large, airtight jar
White vinegar
Sieve
Measuring jug
Boiled and cooled water
A bottle with a spray top

Over several weeks, collect your citrus peel in a small bag in the freezer (this keeps it fresh), being sure to cut away any remaining flesh, just leaving the pith and zest.

Once you've collected a good bagful, decant the peel into a large, airtight jar and cover it completely with vinegar.

Leave the citrus and vinegar jar to brew for about two weeks in a cool, dark place – the vinegar will take on the colour of the peel, and will smell strongly of citrus.

Strain the vinegar into a measuring jug. Top up with the same amount again of boiled and cooled (or distilled) water to dilute it.

Decant into a bottle with a spray top and use as desired for cleaning.

Tip

— Add further scent to your spray by steeping evergreen herbs such as rosemary or bay leaves in the mixture, or even some pine clippings from your Christmas tree.

Marmalade and Chocolate Shortbread

You might not think of marmalade as Scottish, but it was the Keiller family of Dundee who popularised the preserve as we know it in the late eighteenth century, originally selling it in their shop, then opening a factory. In the cold, dark months, the citrus zing of marmalade brings sunshine to the breakfast table – but also to bakes.

As well as eating my veggie haggis, neeps and tatties in a traditional Burns Night Supper, I tend to bake shortbread to celebrate the Scottish bard at the end of January and this twist on the traditional recipe is one I enjoy into early spring. Here, the rich, buttery, citrus shortbread is given sharpness from the marmalade peel and just the right amount of sweetness from the chocolate. Be warned: a batch has been known to disappear in a little over 24 hours in this house...

Makes 16–20

100g fridge-cold butter
150g plain flour
50g caster sugar
50g milk chocolate, chopped into small chunks.
30g marmalade, any big pieces of peel chopped finely

In a large bowl, rub the butter into the flour and sugar with your fingertips until the butter is evenly distributed and the mixture has the texture of breadcrumbs. Add the chocolate and marmalade and mix until the pieces of chocolate and peel are well distributed through the dough.

Bring the mixture together into a ball and lightly knead it, then roll it into a rough sausage shape around 20cm long. Wrap the dough in clingfilm and refrigerate it for 30 minutes–1 hour.

Preheat the oven to 180°C/Fan 160°C/Gas Mark 4 and line two baking trays with baking parchment. Remove the dough from the fridge and chop it into approximately twenty 1cm thick rounds using a sharp knife.

Place the rounds 2cm apart on the prepared trays and bake for 12–14 minutes, until golden. The shortbread will still be a little soft to the touch but will firm up as it cools. Leave to cool on the trays for a few minutes, then pop the shortbread onto a wire rack to cool completely.

Tip

— Store your shortbread in an airtight container and finish it within a few days. It goes soft more quickly than your standard shortbread thanks to the added moisture from the marmalade.

Blood Orange Drizzle Loaf

Using seasonal ingredients and being led and inspired by them in the kitchen is one of the key ways in which I embrace the darkness of this time of year. Citrus season seems to arrive just when we need it at the end of winter, adding bright and zesty colour and flavour to all manner of makes and bakes. This blood orange drizzle loaf is a cross between an upside-down cake and a drizzle cake: a moist, orange-flecked sponge topped with slightly caramelised fruit, and covered with a zesty blood orange drizzle.

Serves 10

180g slightly salted butter, softened (or unsalted butter and a pinch of salt), plus extra for greasing
180g caster sugar
2 blood oranges, zested, then peeled and the flesh sliced into 5mm rounds
3 large free-range eggs
150g self-raising flour
30g ground almonds

For the drizzle:

100g caster sugar
2 blood oranges, zest and juice

Grease a 900g loaf tin and line it with baking paper. Preheat the oven to 180°C/Fan 160°C/Gas Mark 4.

In the bowl of a stand mixer, or by hand in a large bowl with a wooden spoon, cream the butter, sugar and blood orange zest together until light and fluffy. Beat in the eggs one at a time with a little flour, then fold in the rest of the flour.

Fold the ground almonds into the mixture. The batter will be quite stiff (it needs to be to soak up all the lovely drizzle coming its way after baking).

Place the orange slices in an even layer in the bottom of the lined loaf tin. It's okay if they overlap slightly. Pour the batter on top of the orange slices and gently level the top with a spatula.

Bake for 50–55 minutes, or until golden, risen and a skewer inserted in the middle comes out clean. Leave to cool in the tin for 10 minutes, then turn out, upside down, onto a wire rack so that the orange slices are visible on the top.

While the cake cools slightly, make the drizzle. Mix the caster sugar with the zest and juice of the blood oranges. Poke holes in the top of the cake with a skewer and, placing a plate underneath the rack to catch drips, pour the drizzle over the top a little at a time, waiting for it to absorb between additions.

Leave to cool completely, then cut into slices to serve.

Tip

— The cake tastes even better after a couple of days because the drizzle keeps it so moist, but it's best kept in the fridge.

Pressed Flower Botanical Notebook

A big part of embracing the darkness is knowing that it isn't forever, that brighter days are coming. Waretym is the perfect moment to make some gentle plans for the lighter half of the year to help keep this in mind, particularly on dark days when it feels like winter is interminable. Decorating a notebook, journal or planner with pressed flowers is a way to get inspired for the season ahead, whether using it to put dates in the diary for garden visits or to plot out your own garden for the floral seasons.

Paper crafts are filled with nostalgia, taking me back to covering jotters for school and making mood boards to decorate notebooks and sketchbooks. There's something really therapeutic about the repetitive action of cutting and sticking, and I always think plans are all the more inspiring when they're packaged in something beautiful. You could use pressed flowers that you already have, or make some new ones with snowdrops, daffodils or other early spring flowers, pressed flat between greaseproof paper in a flower press or under a heavy stack of books for a week or two.

You will need:

- Paper that is just over double the width of the notebook, plus its spine (textured paper such as sugar paper is good)
- A plain notebook
- Scissors
- Eco-friendly glue
- Pressed flowers

First, cut out your paper: you want to make sure that the paper is exactly the height of your notebook, and wide enough to fit the whole cover, with a bit of excess to tuck into the front and back.

Wrap the paper around the book, pressing it down along the spine and edges, then fold and tuck it in at the front and back.

Remove the paper and cover the inside in a thin layer of glue, then attach the paper to the notebook.

Now the fun bit: arrange your pressed flowers in your desired design on the front of the notebook. Glue your pressed flowers into place, making sure to use enough glue to stick any small leaves or twiddly bits of plant down, but not so much that you have gluey marks all over your notebook.

Repeat for the back and the spine. Leave to dry standing up completely before using.

Tip

— If you want to make your decorated notebook sturdier, then you may wish to cover it with some environmentally friendly, see-through self-adhesive covering.

A FINAL GLIMMER

As I write to you now, it's almost exactly two years since I gave birth to the baby whose pregnancy I chart in these pages. The early days of motherhood have not been without their challenges, but the glimmers have been plentiful, and I hold them closer than ever.

This book has been one of those glimmers. I started tending the seeds of this idea when my son was around three months old. *Gloaming* has been written in the twenty-minute snatches throughout his first autumn and winter when – if! – he napped. So, if all you have is twenty minutes to dip in and out of this book and seek glimmers with my guidance, that it is enough. Those glimmers start adding up if we notice and nurture them.

Whatever our season of life, dark times might consume us for a while. Sometimes things feel difficult because they are difficult. Winters can be long and dark and deeper than we might ever imagine. But we can find glimmers of light in the gloaming. We can reconnect with our surroundings and their stories. We can kindle our creativity and keep it sacred. Sometimes the faintest light is the most vital of all.

INDEX

ACKNOWLEDGEMENTS

To my wonderful readers, thank you. Conversations on my first book tour informed the direction of Gloaming; I hope it helps you navigate dark times. Thank you to my lovely Substack community and recipe testers for your helpful feedback. Thank you to everyone who has supported my seasonal gatherings, whether attending, spreading the word, sharing their spaces and more.

Thank you to the whole team at Bloomsbury and everyone involved in the making of this book, especially my editor Samhita Foria. To my literary agent Megan Staunton and the team at Bergstrom Studio for always cheering me on. To Kitty Stogdon for the thought and care you put into everything you do. To the talented Lucy Sykes-Thompson and Flora Dewar who brought the book to life so beautifully. To all the amazing booksellers, lifestyle shops and creative businesses who have supported my books.

Thank you to my creative pals, especially Marion, florist extraordinaire who always goes the extra mile; Jemma for your attention to detail and web wizardry; Jess for the walks with P and L and foodie chats; and Alannah for your knowledge and boosting my confidence as I pivoted career. To Kerri and the Oak Mothers: you've followed and celebrated this book right from the start. Thank you for hearing and holding me.

Thank you to my midwife Carol for your kind care and to Melanie, Ronnie and Sarah for your support that goes beyond words.

To our family, especially Gadan and Mimi, Maymie and Laur-Laur, Gan Gan, Nana and Kiki. Thank you for everything. Thank you to Gran and Granda who we miss and think of often, and whose memory inspires my love of nature and creativity.

To Al and Laurie, who this book is dedicated to. Al, thank you for being my first reader, for doing the juggle with me, for all the workshops past and present, for all the walks and adventures, for all you do for our family. Thank you for always holding my pieces. Laurie, the majority of this book was written with you at my side from when you were a tiny three-month old, and this book is all the more special because we did it together. It's yours too. Thank you for your smiles, your sense of humour, your empathy and your love. You inspire me every day. The 'wowl' in this book is for you. We love you so much.

Rosie Steer is an author and creative who lives in Edinburgh. She is the author of *Slow Seasons: A Creative Guide to Reconnecting with Nature the Celtic Way* (Bloomsbury, 2023) filled with recipes, crafts and activities inspired by the Celtic Wheel of the Year. Rosie hosts seasonal gatherings, workshops and retreats that celebrate nature's rhythms through craft, cooking and community. She shares ways to slow down and embrace seasonal living on Instagram and Substack, @everythinglooksrosie.

BLOOMSBURY PUBLISHING
Bloomsbury Publishing Plc
50 Bedford Square, London, WC1B 3DP, UK
29 Earlsfort Terrace, Dublin 2, D02 AY28, Ireland

First published in Great Britain 2026

A catalogue record for this book is available from the British Library

Library of Congress Cataloguing-in-Publication data has been applied for

ISBN: HB: 978-1-5266-9492-8;
eBook: 978-1-5266-9491-1

10 9 8 7 6 5 4 3 2 1

Commissioning Editor: Samhita Foria
Project Editor: Kitty Stogdon
Designer: Studio Polka
Illustrator: Flora Dewar
Production: Laura Brodie

Printed in China by Toppan Leefung Printing Ltd

MIX
Paper | Supporting responsible forestry
FSC www.fsc.org FSC® C104723

To find out more about our authors and books visit www.bloomsbury.com and sign up for our newsletters. For product safety related questions contact productsafety@bloomsbury.com